TATTOO

Sketchbook and Journal VI

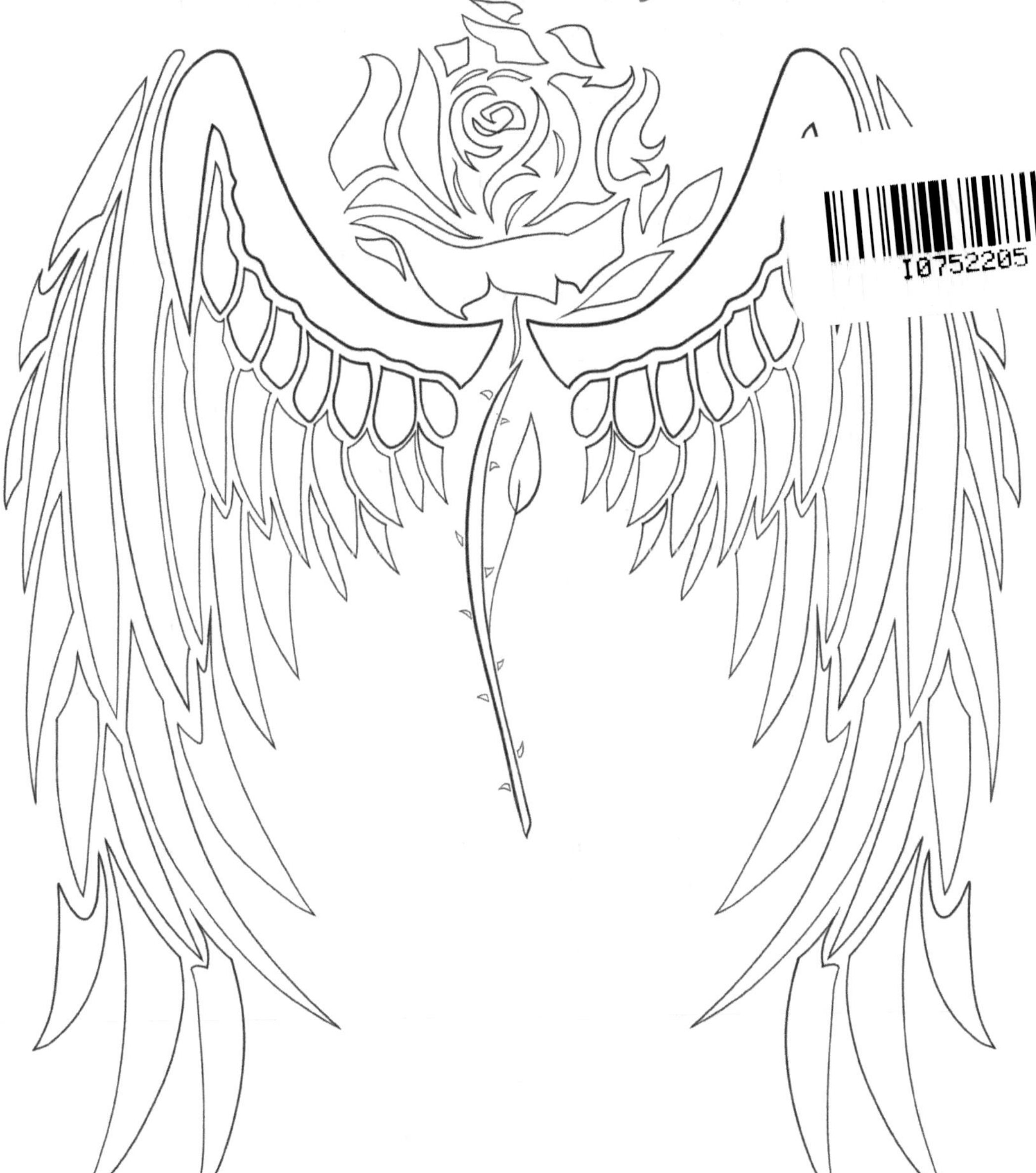

By Tangie Marie and Cameron Purvis

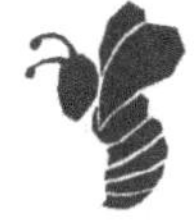

Be Amazing, LLC Publishing
Youngsville, Louisiana
First Edition, December 2020

Published by Be Amazing, LLC Publishing,
Youngsville, Louisiana

ISBN 978-1-7360796-4-5 (Paperback)

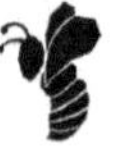

Be Amazing, LLC Publishing
Youngsville, Louisiana
First Edition, December 2020

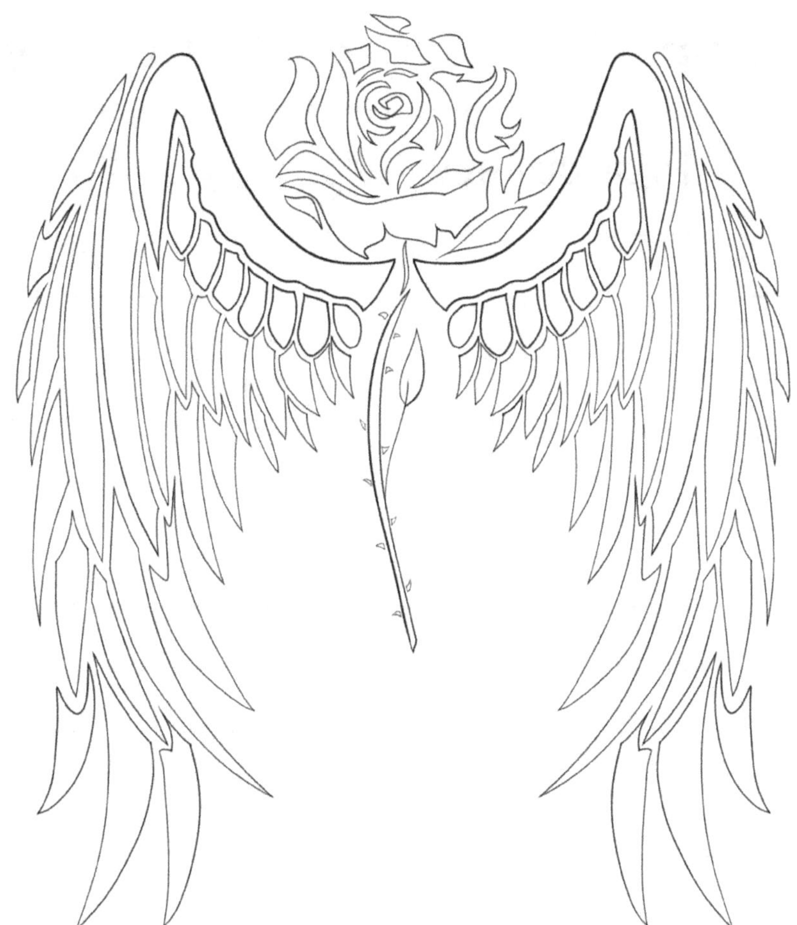

This Tattoo Sketchbook and Journal VI
Belongs To:

Tattoo Sketchbook and Journal VI Table of Contents

Project Title	Page(s)

Tattoo Sketchbook and Journal VI Table of Contents

Project Title	Page(s)

Tattoo Sketchbook and Journal VI Table of Contents

Project Title	Page(s)

Tattoo Sketchbook and Journal VI Table of Contents

Project Title	Page(s)

Client Name:

Placement:

Theme:

Planned Date:

Palette

Design:

Details / Notes:

Name ______________________________ Date ____________________

Front View Head/Neck Sketch Template

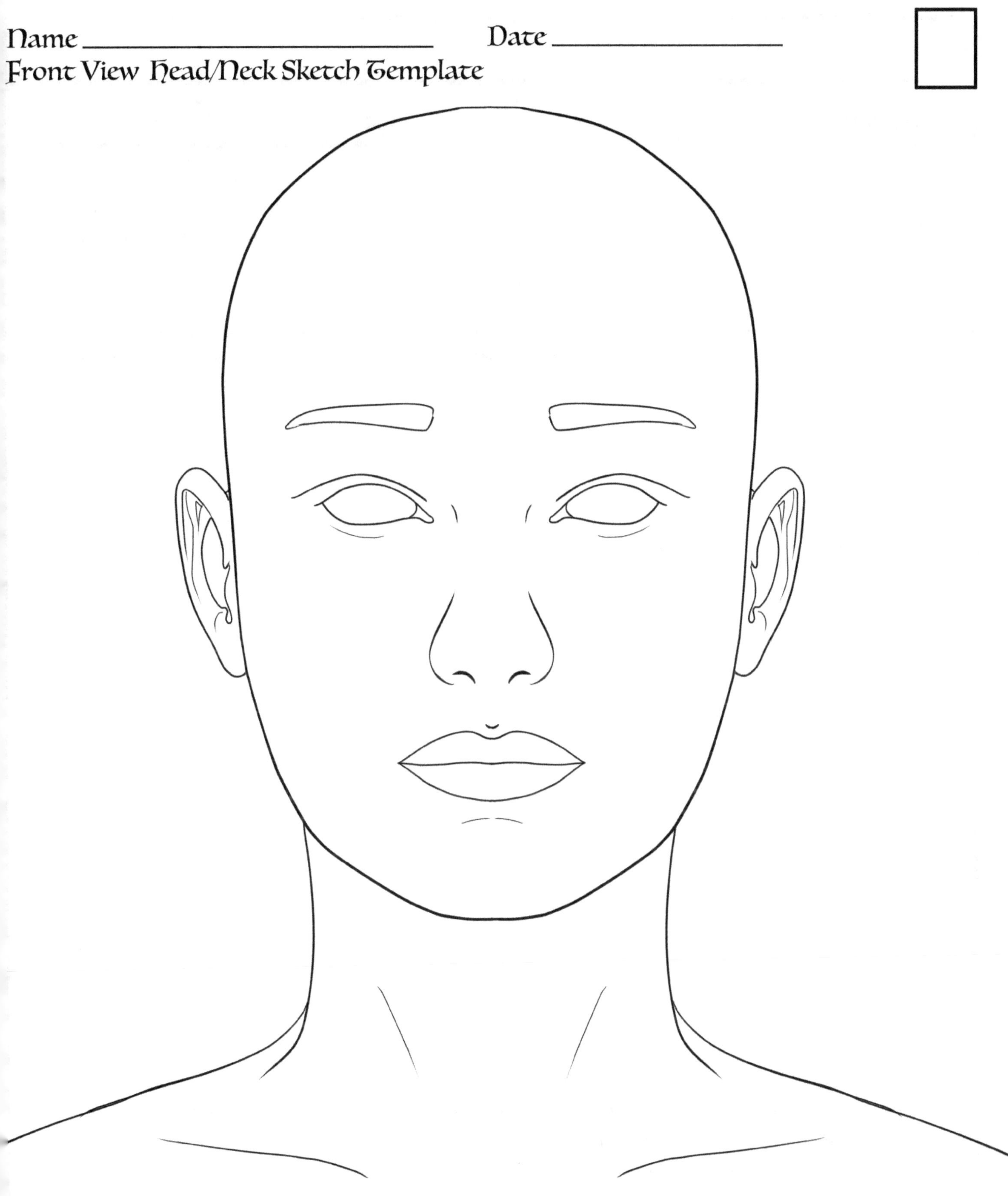

Client Name:

Placement:

Theme:

Planned Date:

Palette

Design:

Details / Notes:

Name ______________________________ Date ____________________

Front View Head/Neck Sketch Template

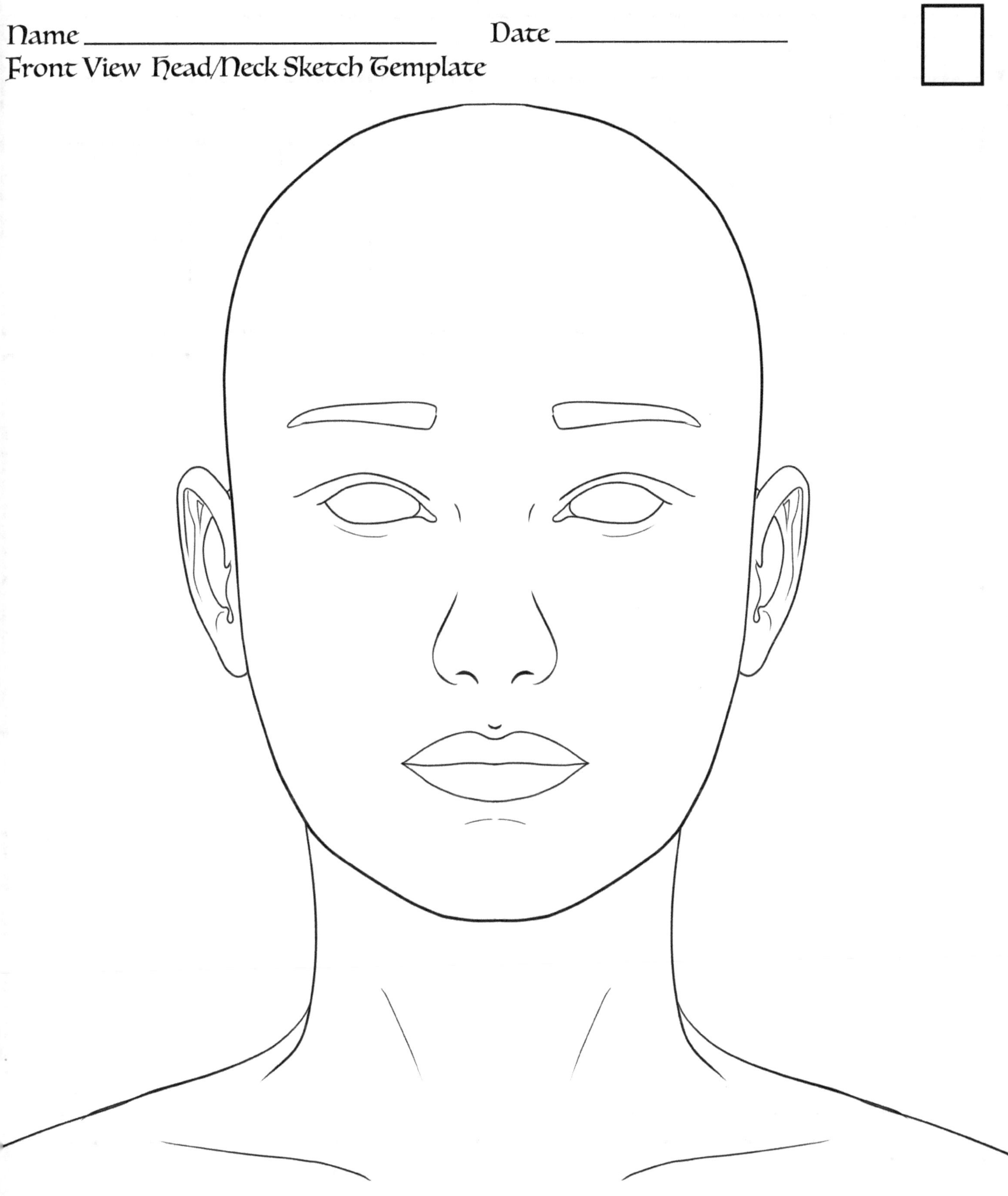

Client Name:

Placement:

Theme:

Planned Date:

Palette

Design:

Details / Notes:

Name ______________________________ Date ____________________

Front View Head/Neck Sketch Template

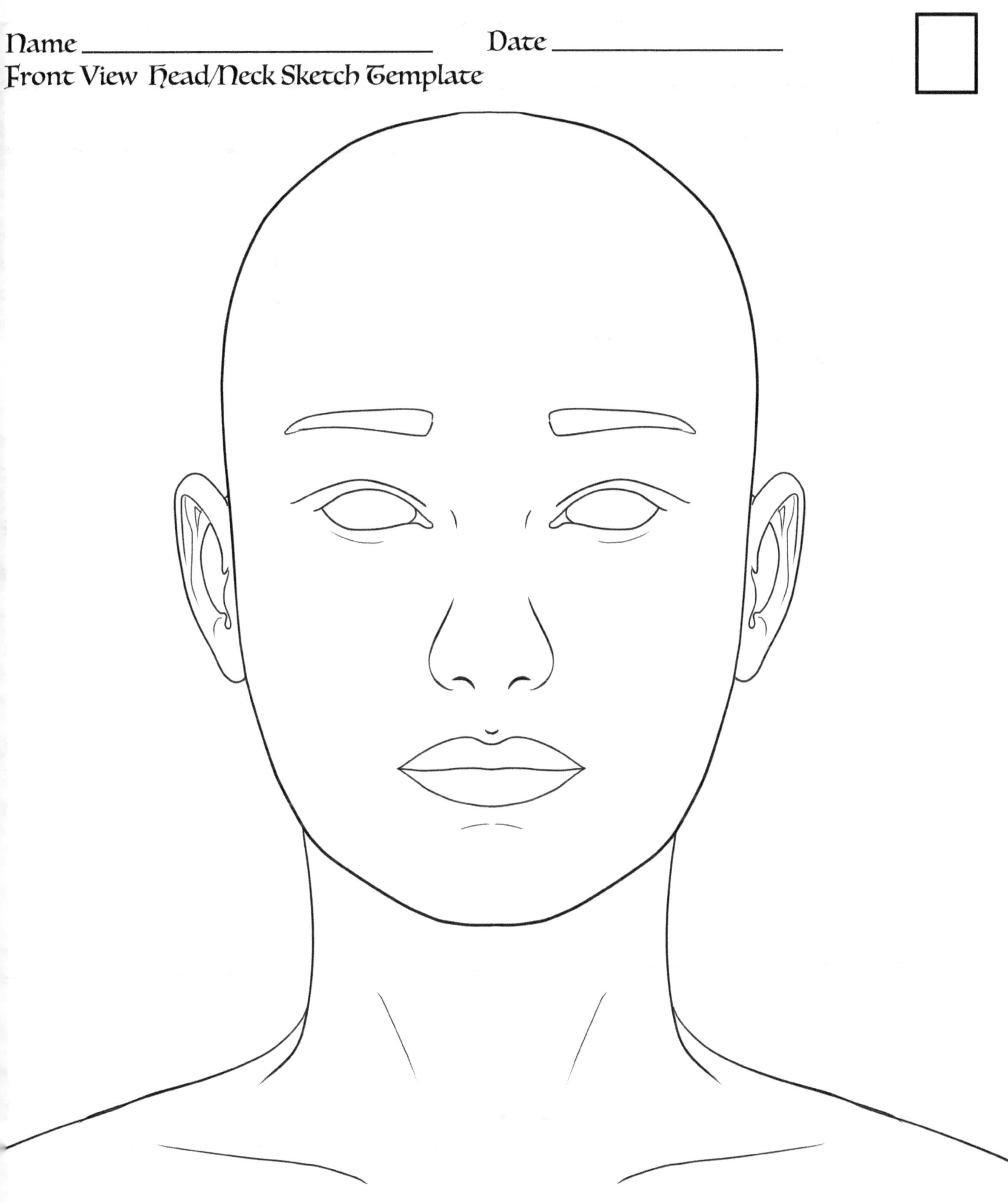

Client Name:

Placement:	Palette
Theme:	
Planned Date:	

Design:

Details / Notes:

Name ______________________________ Date ____________________

Front View Head/Neck Sketch Template

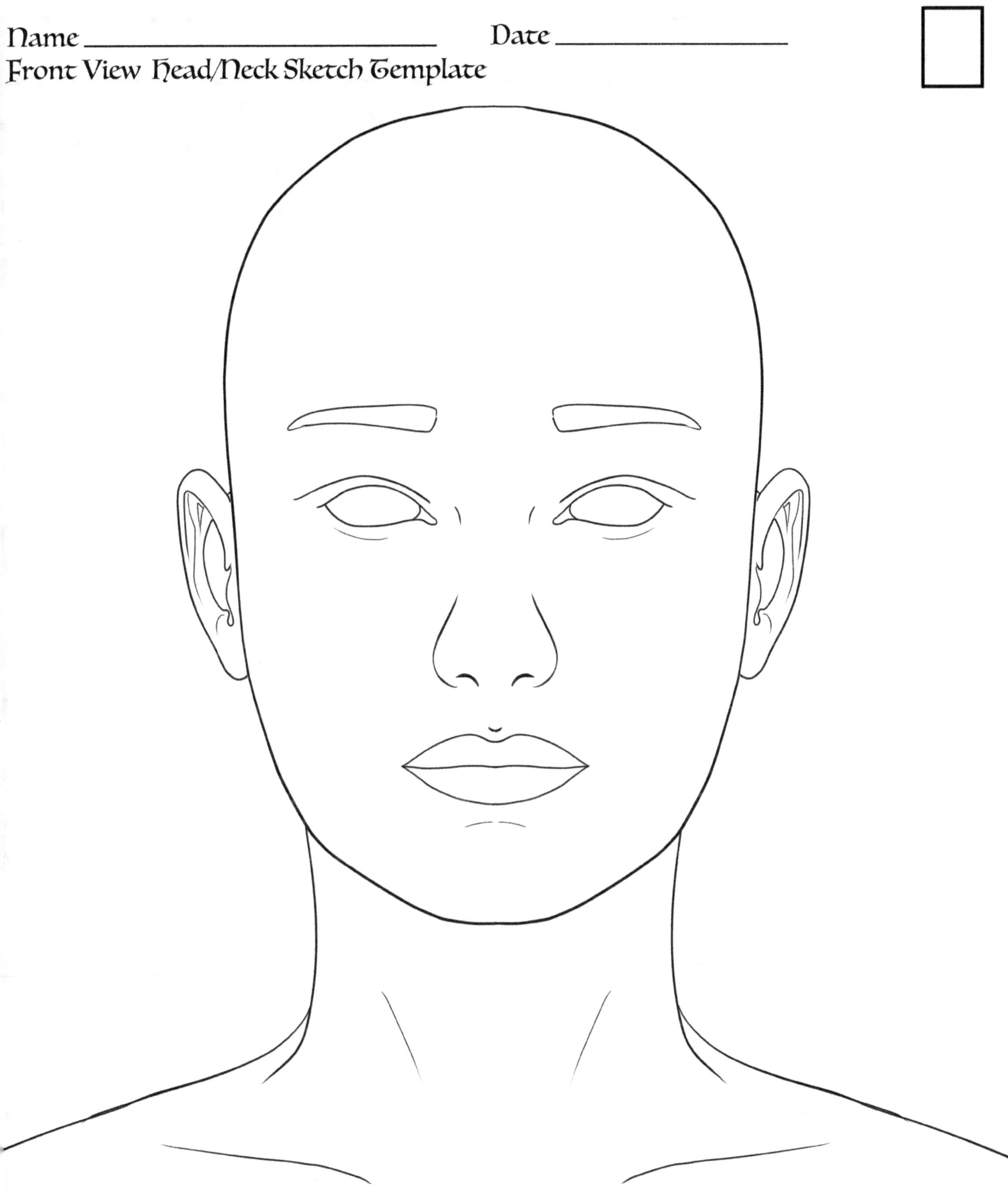

Client Name:

Placement:

Palette

Theme:

Planned Date:

Design:

Details / Notes:

Name ______________________________ Date ____________________

Front View Head/Neck Sketch Template

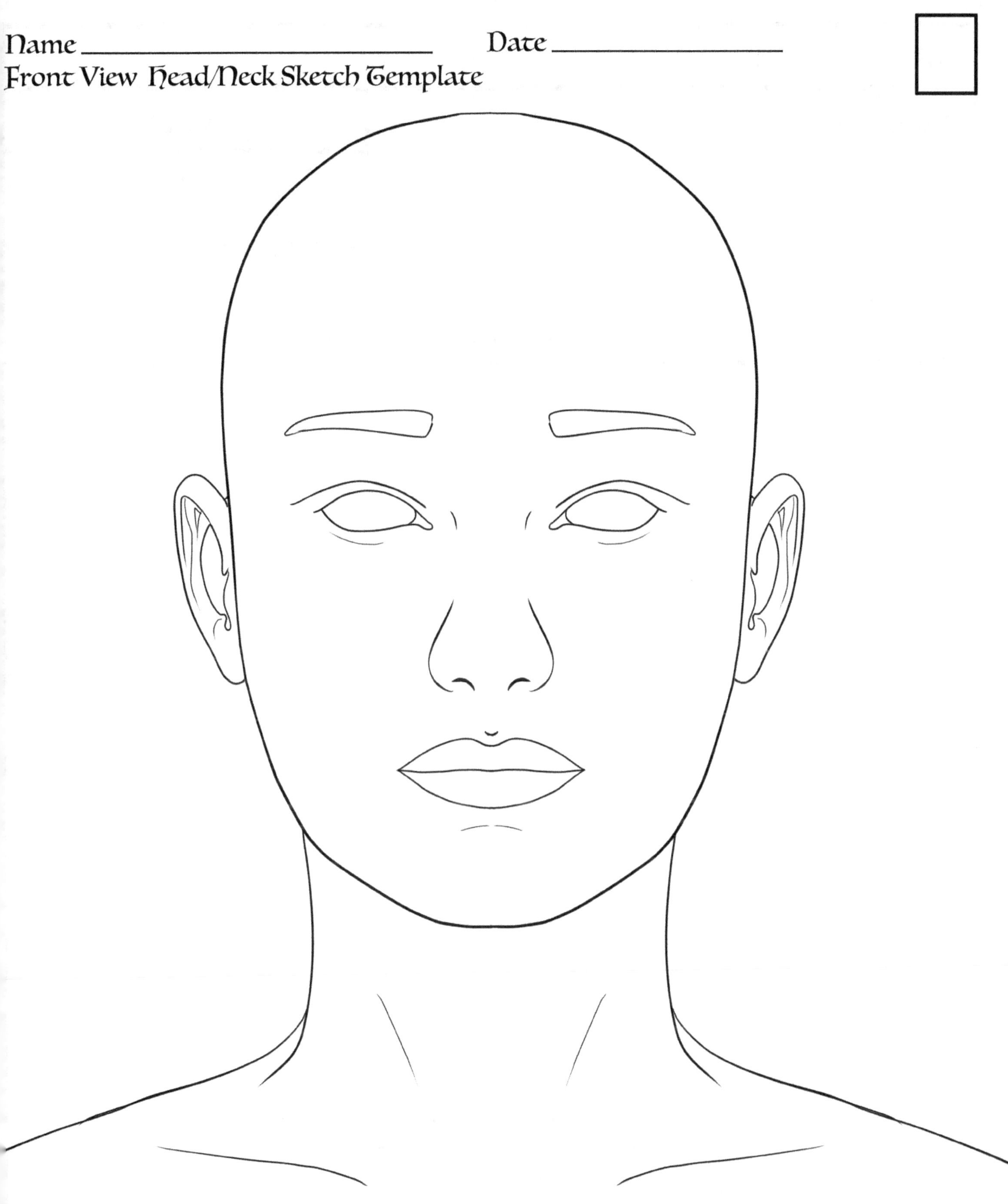

Client Name:

Placement:

Palette

Theme:

Planned Date:

Design:

Details / Notes:

Name ______________________________ Date ____________________

Front View Head/Neck Sketch Template

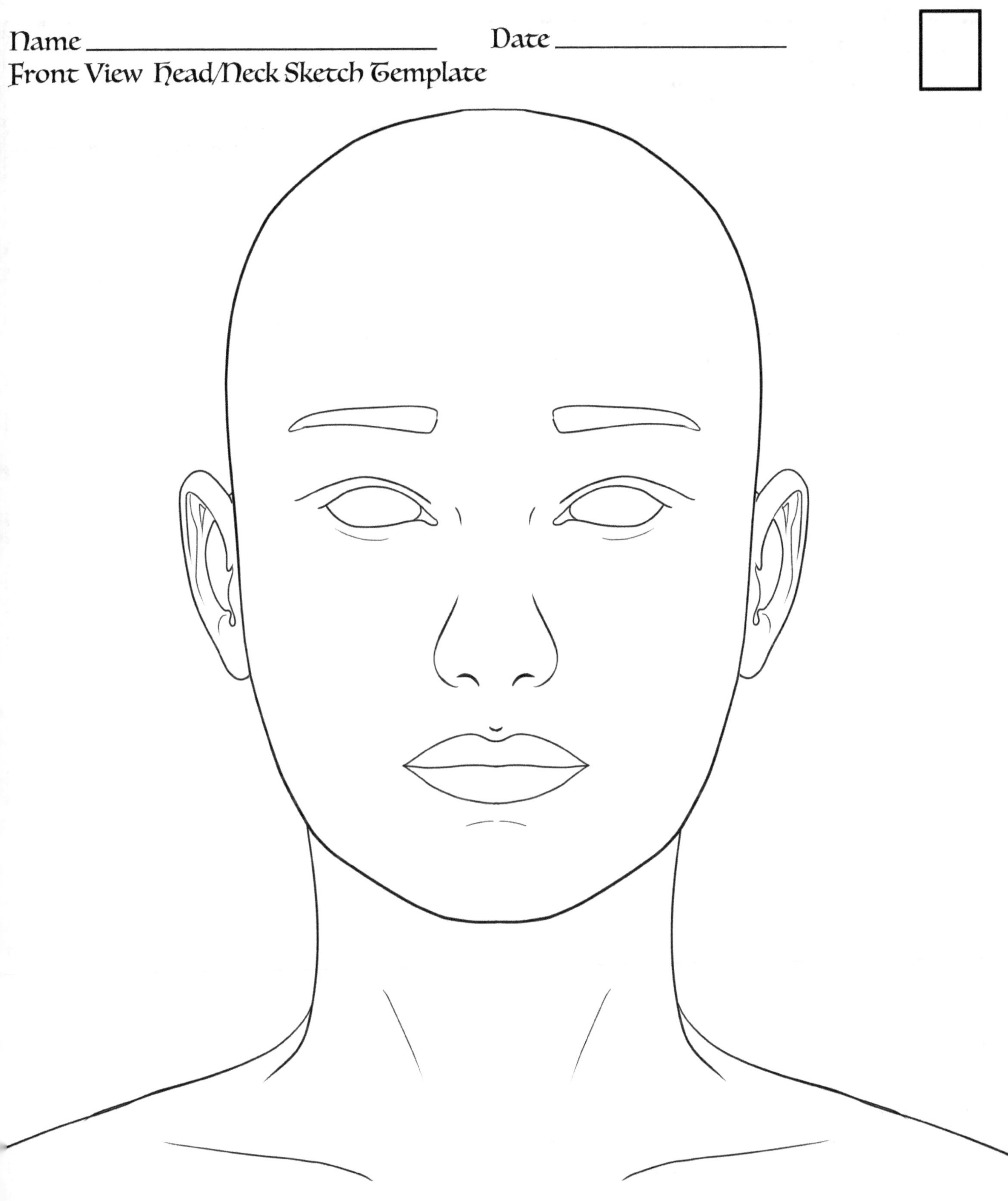

Client Name:

Placement:

Theme:

Planned Date:

Palette

Design:

Details / Notes:

Name ______________________ Date ________________

Front View Head/Neck Sketch Template

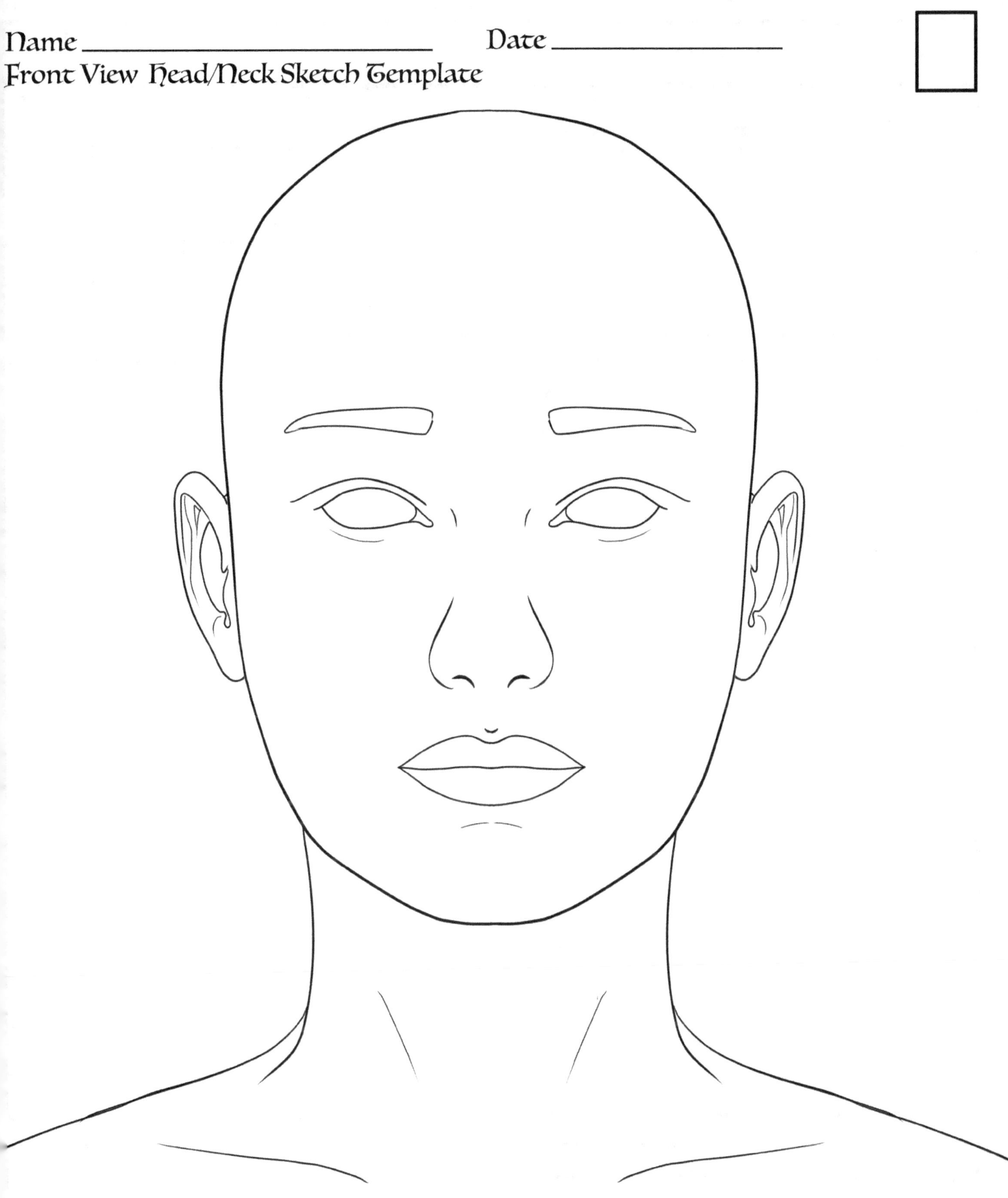

Client Name:

Placement:

Theme:

Planned Date:

Palette

Design:

Details / Notes:

Name ______________________________ Date ____________________

Front View Head/Neck Sketch Template

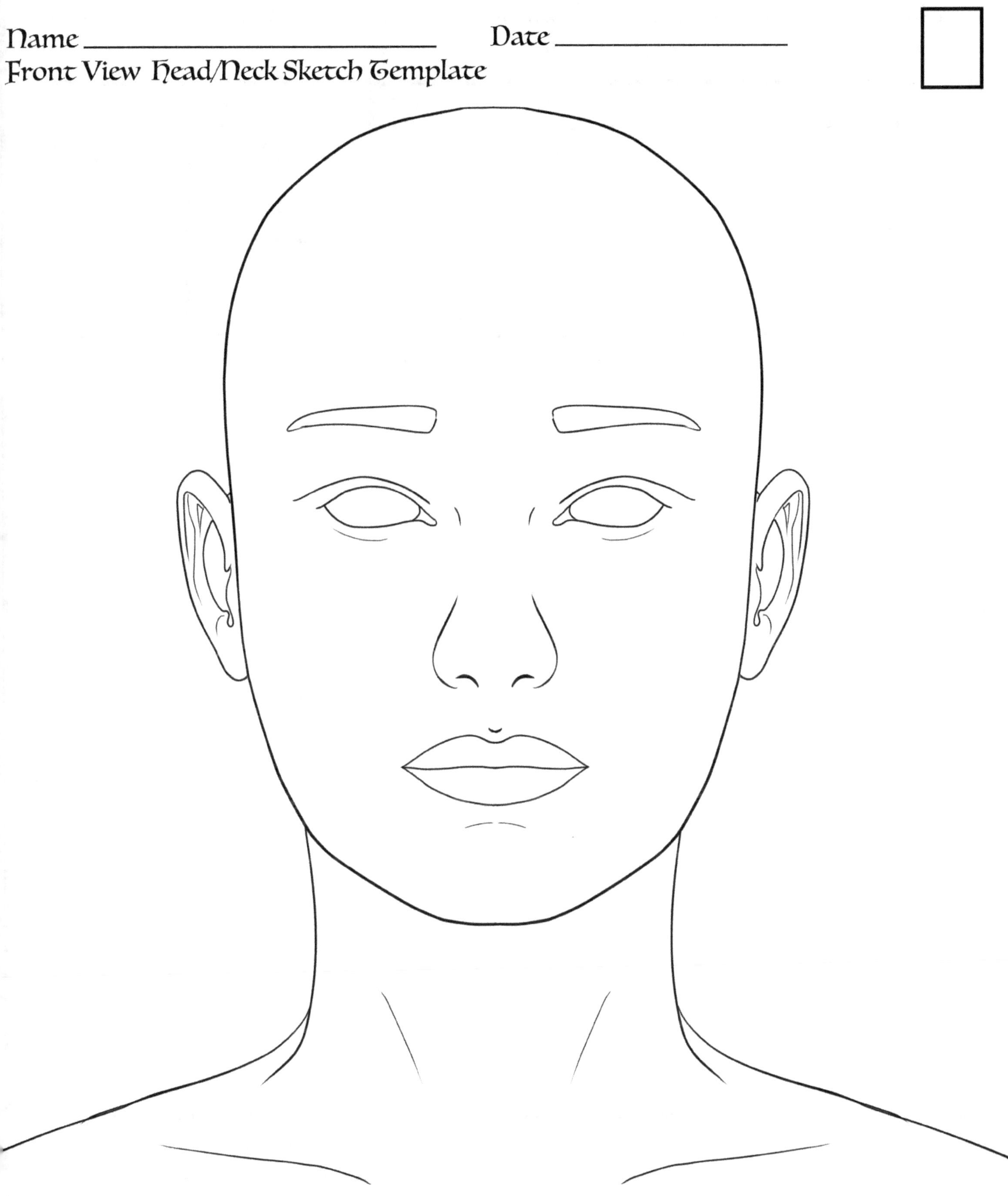

Client Name:

Placement:

Theme:

Planned Date:

Palette

Design:

Details / Notes:

Name ______________________________ Date ____________________

Front View Head/Neck Sketch Template

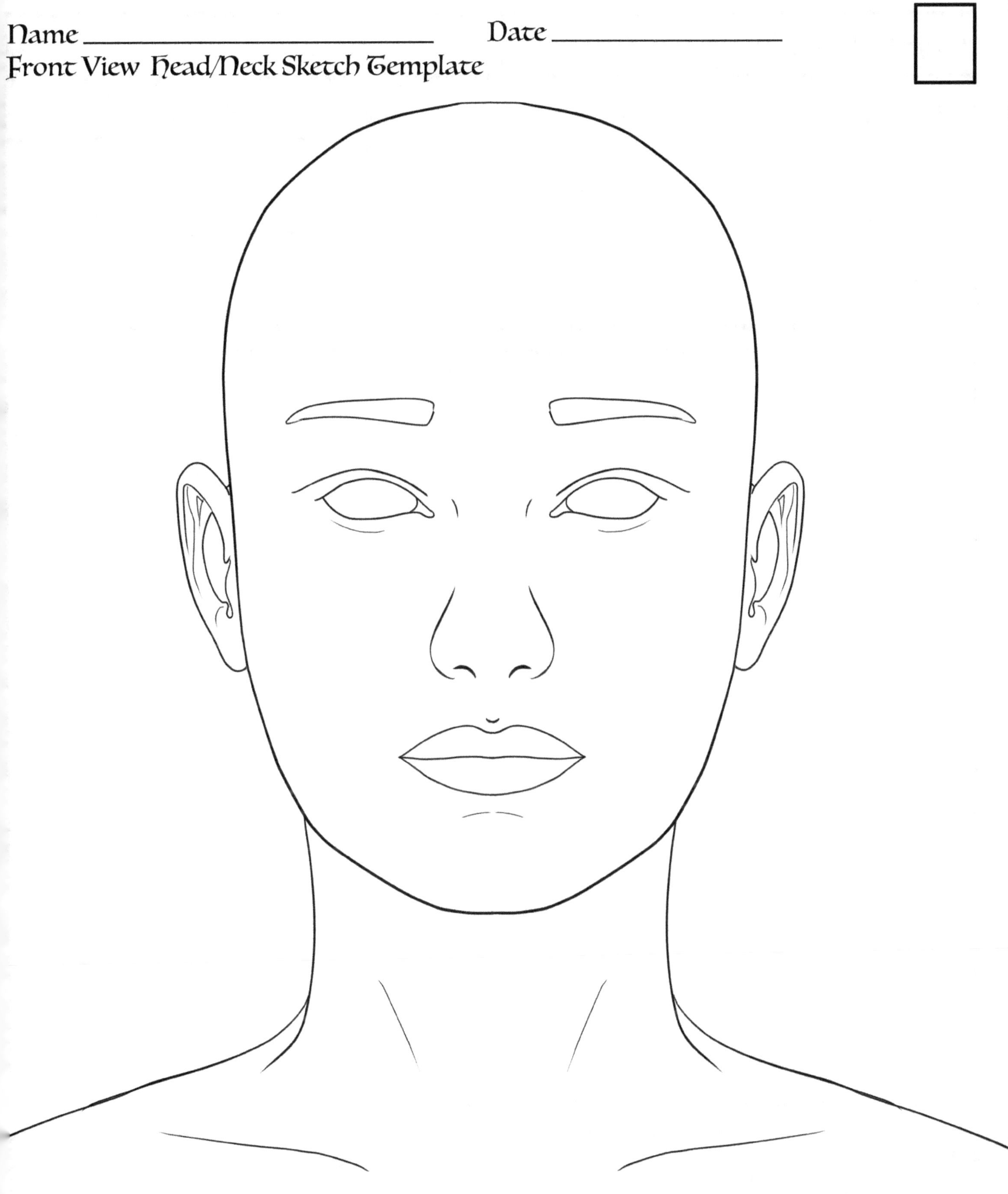

Client Name:

Placement:

Theme:

Planned Date:

Palette

Design:

Details / Notes:

Name ______________________________ Date ____________________

Front View Head/Neck Sketch Template

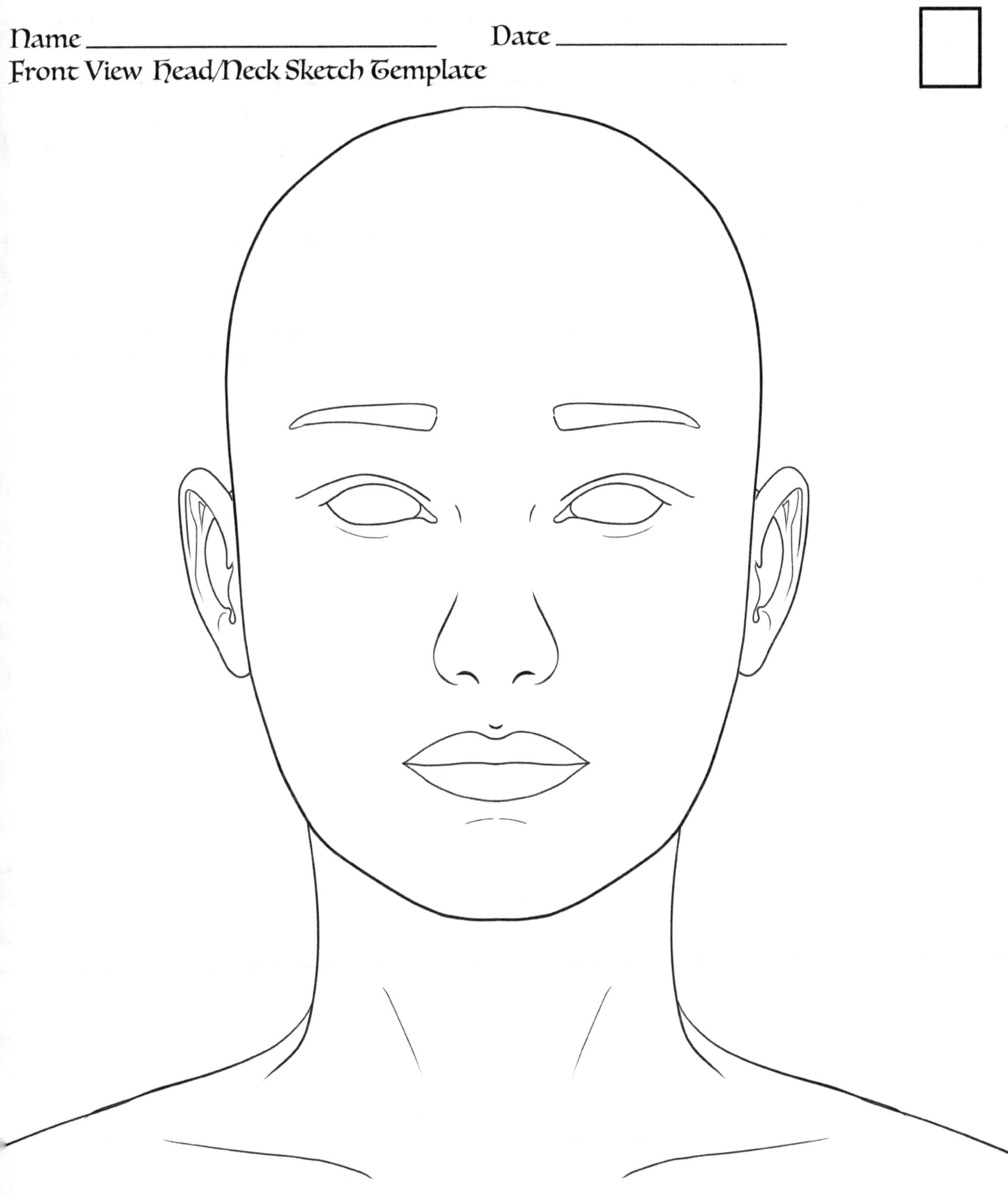

Client Name:

Placement:

Theme:

Planned Date:

Palette

Design:

Details / Notes:

Name ______________________________ Date ____________________

Front View Head/Neck Sketch Template

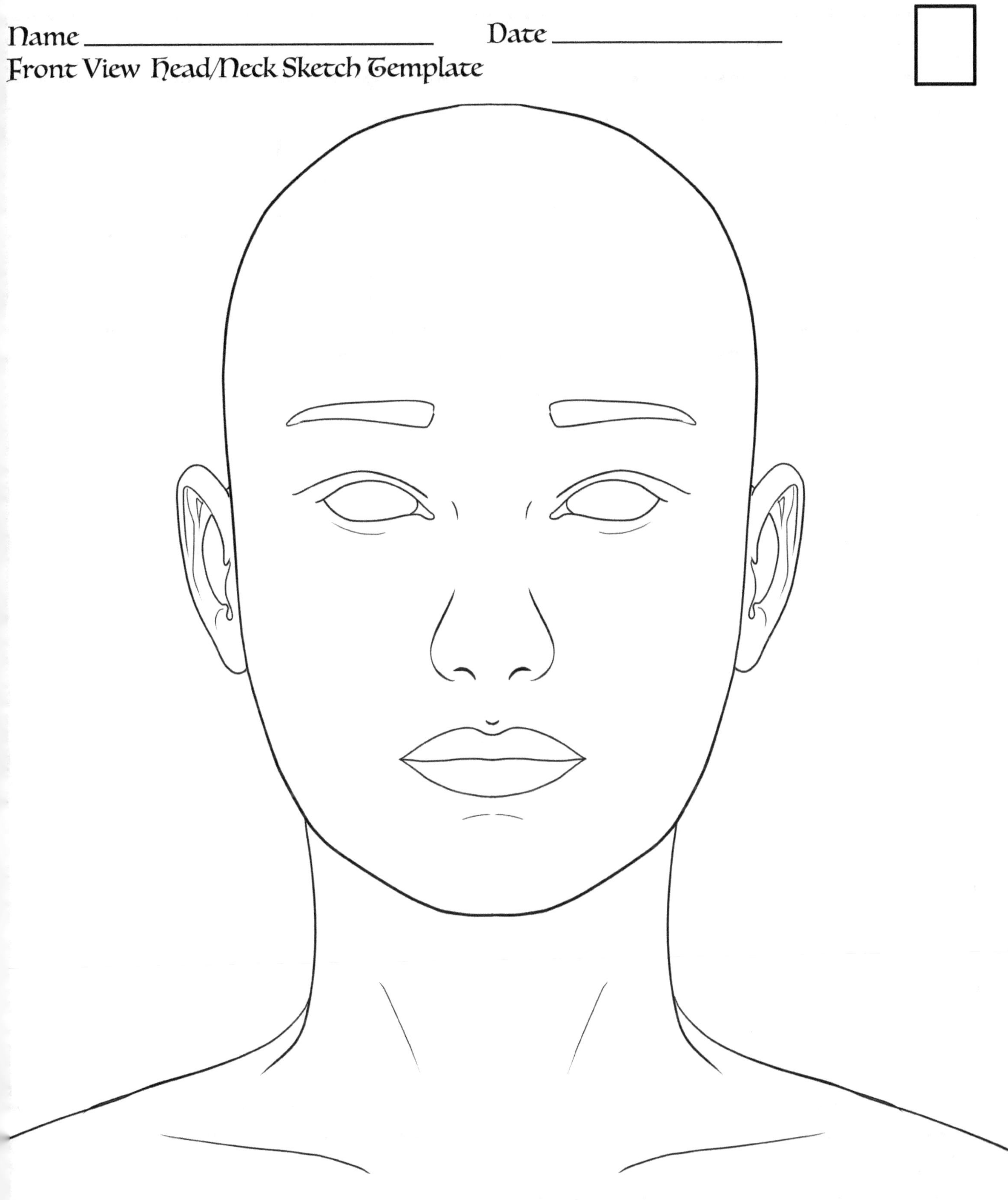

Client Name:

Placement:

Theme:

Planned Date:

Palette

Design:

Details / Notes:

Name ______________________________ Date ____________________

Front View Head/Neck Sketch Template

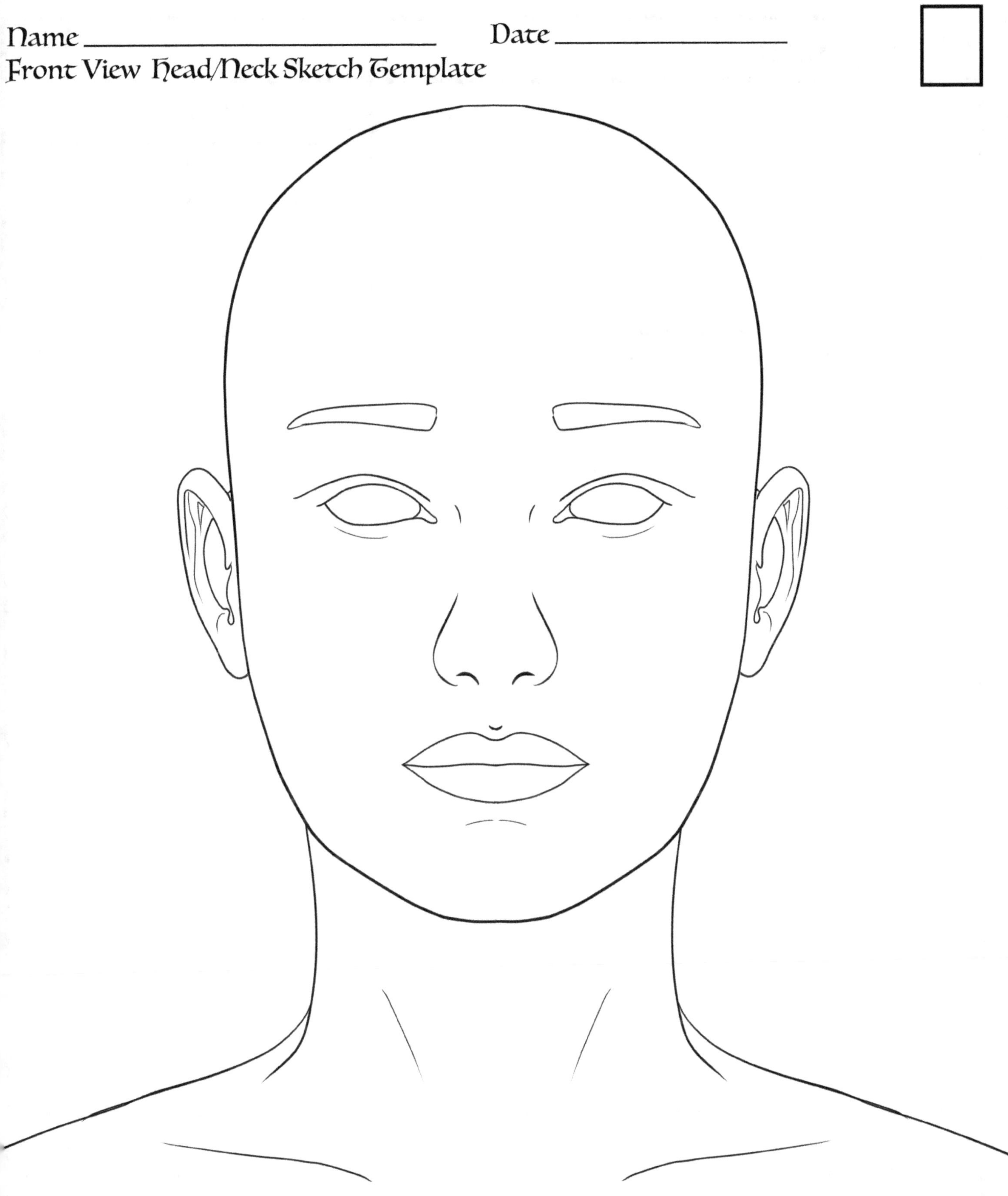

Client Name:

Placement:

Theme:

Planned Date:

Palette

Design:

Details / Notes:

Name ______________________________ Date ____________________

Front View Head/Neck Sketch Template

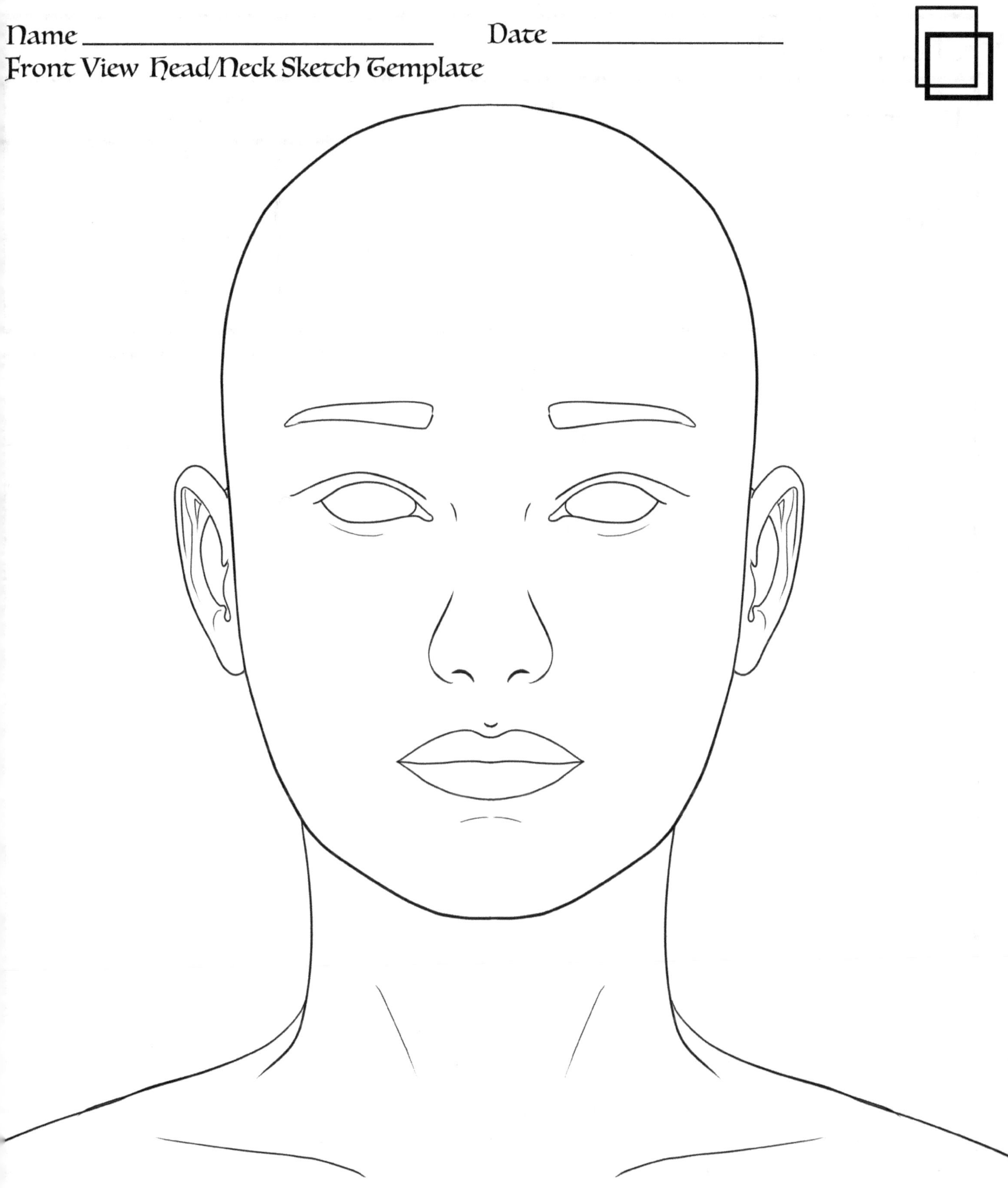

Client Name:

Placement:

Theme:

Planned Date:

Palette

Design:

Details / Notes:

Name ______________________________ Date ____________________

Left Side View Head/Neck Sketch Template

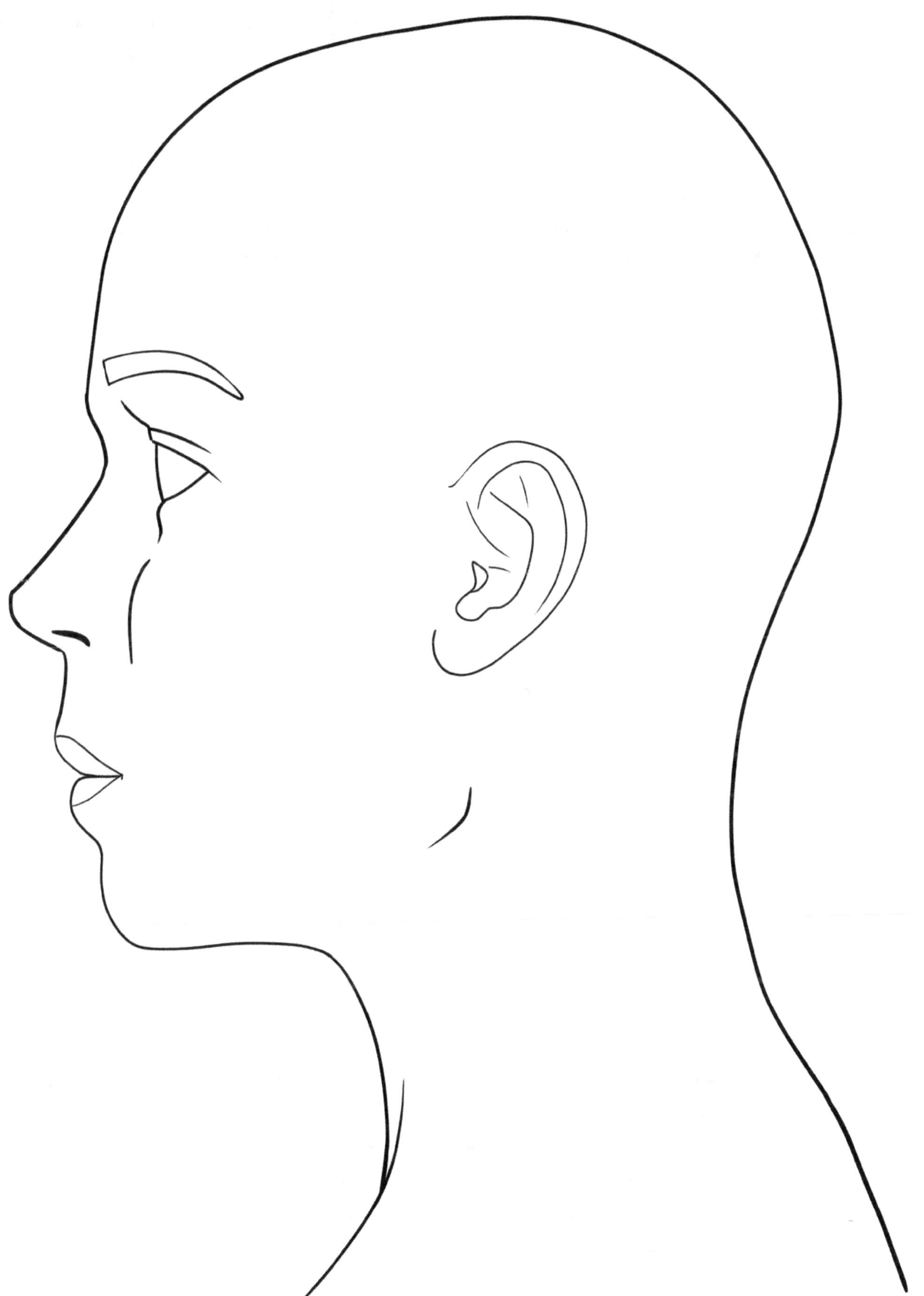

Client Name:

Placement:

Theme:

Planned Date:

Palette

Design:

Details / Notes:

Name ______________________________ Date ____________________

Left Side View Head/Neck Sketch Template

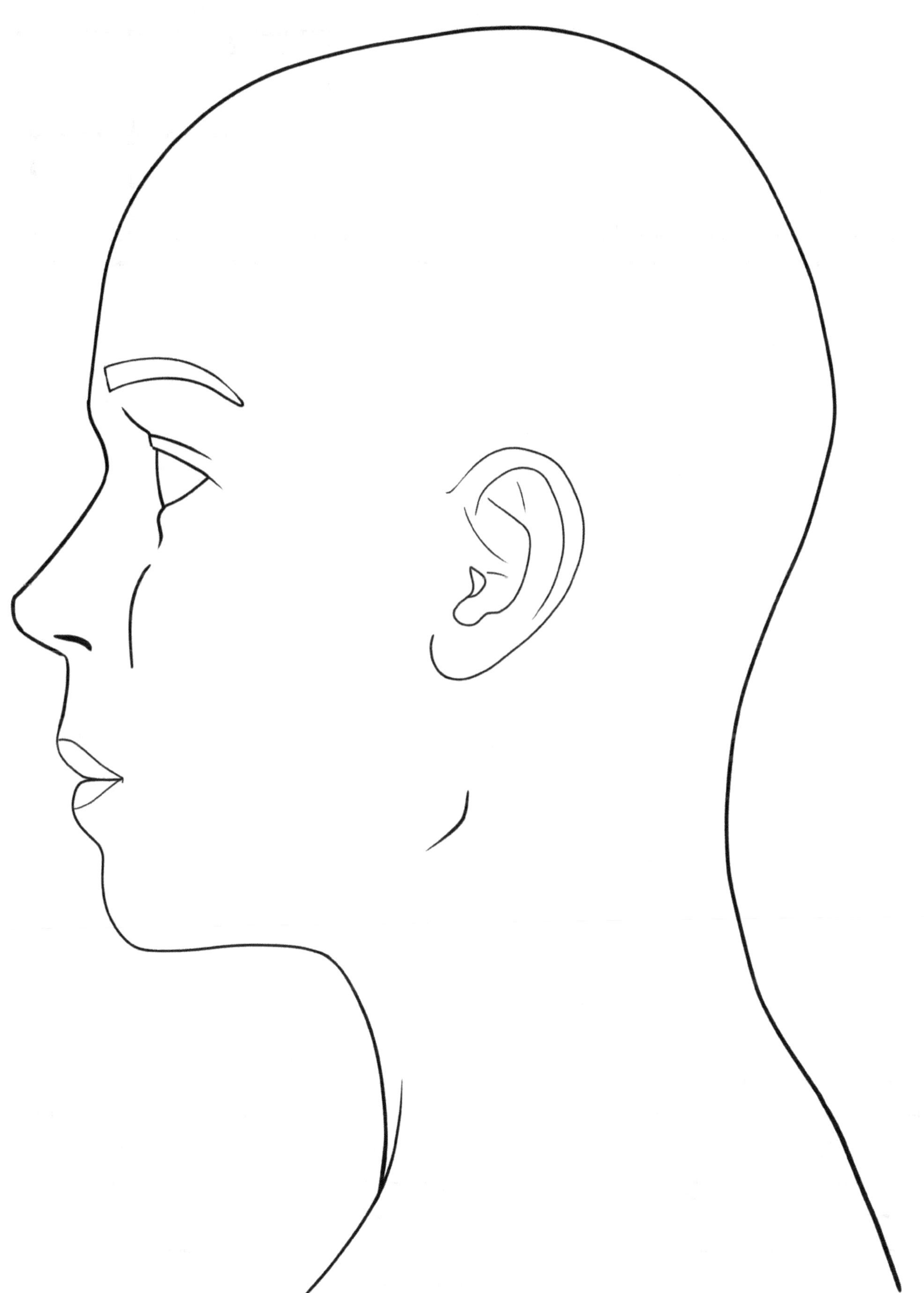

Client Name:

Placement:

Theme:

Planned Date:

Palette

Design:

Details / Notes:

Name ______________________________ Date ____________________

Left Side View Head/Neck Sketch Template

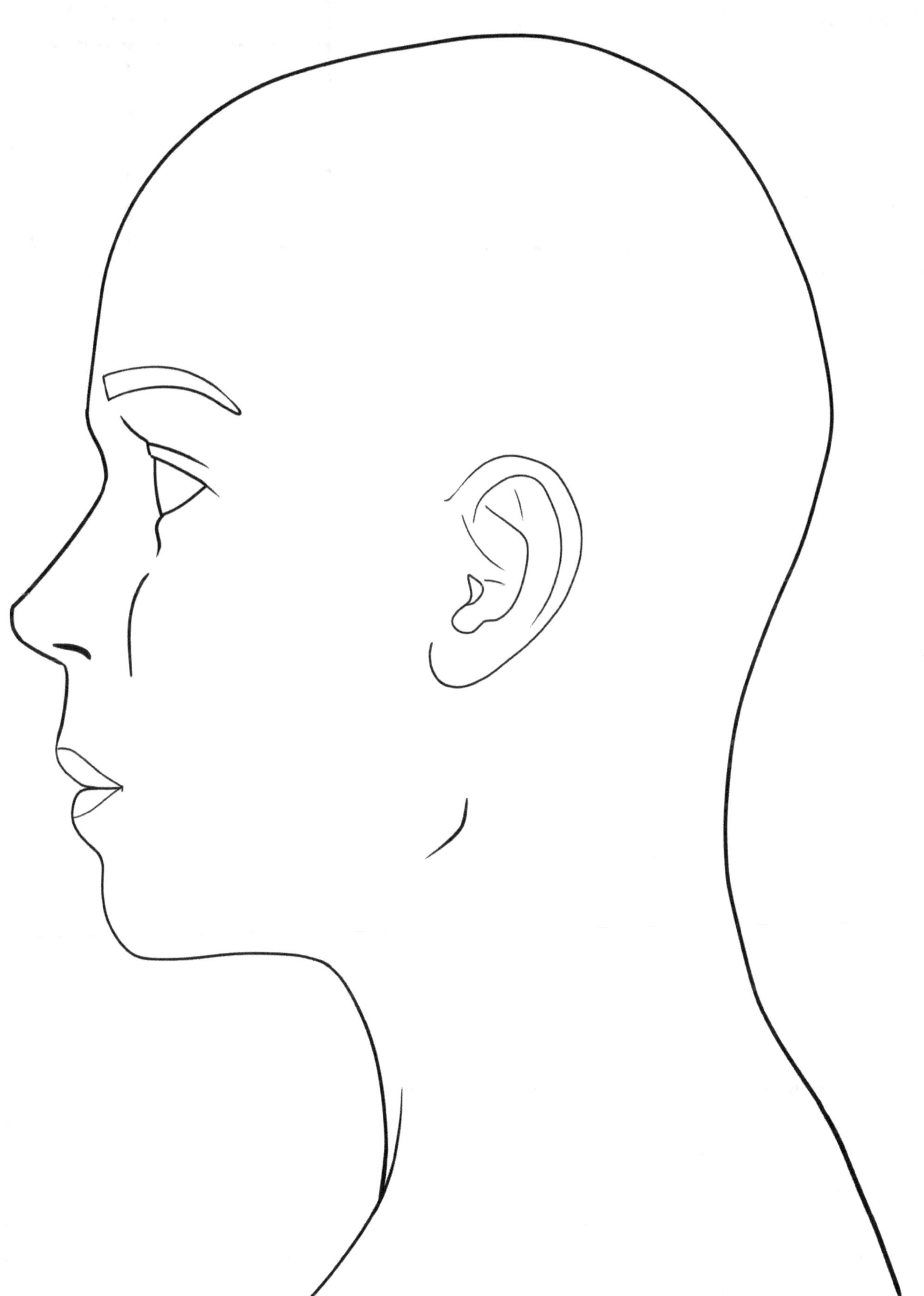

Client Name:	

Placement:	Palette			
Theme:				
Planned Date:				

Design:

Details / Notes:

Name ______________________________ Date ____________________

Left Side View Head/Neck Sketch Template

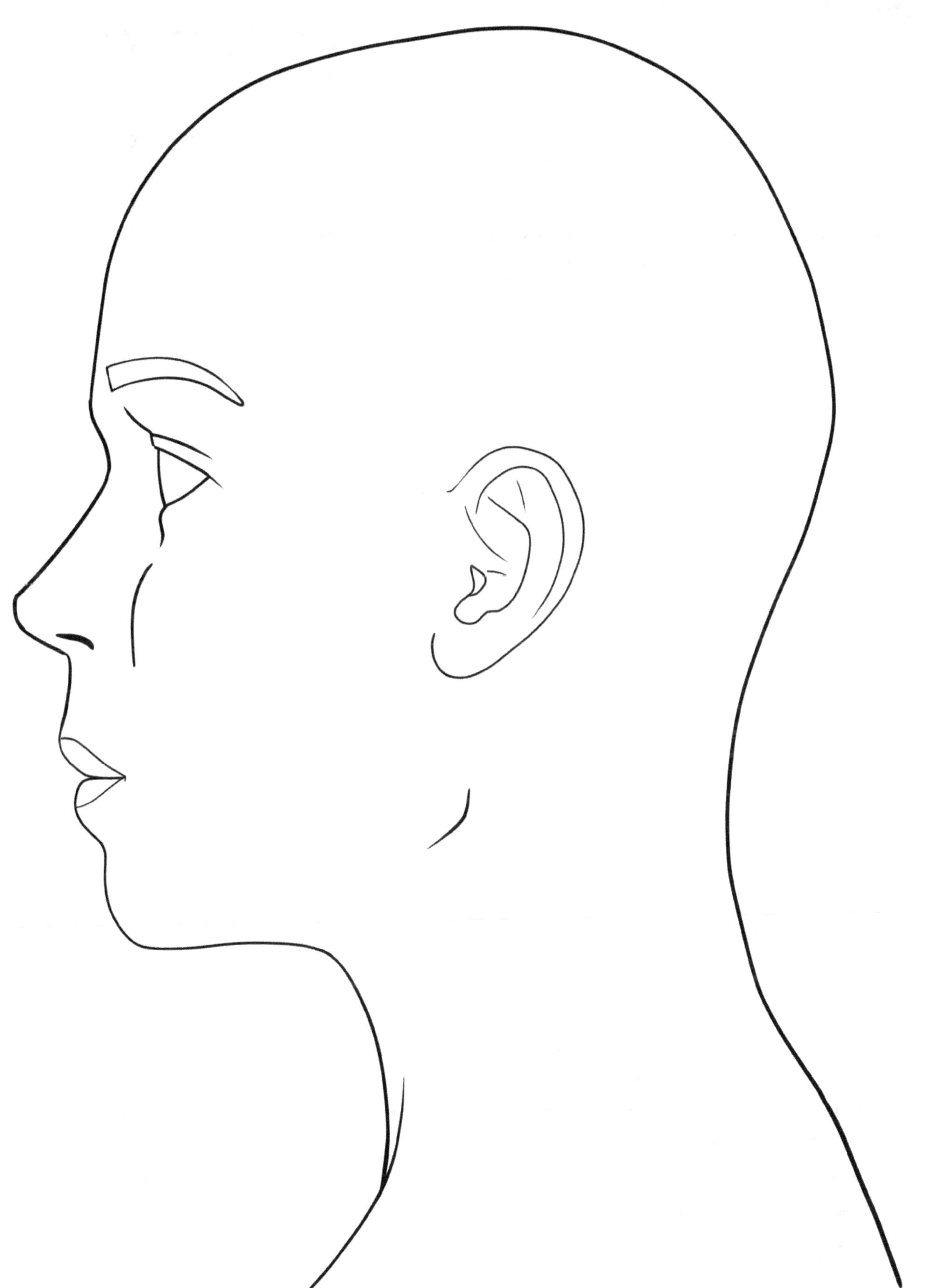

Client Name:

Placement:

Theme:

Planned Date:

Palette

Design:

Details / Notes:

Name ____________________________ Date ____________________

Left Side View Head/Neck Sketch Template

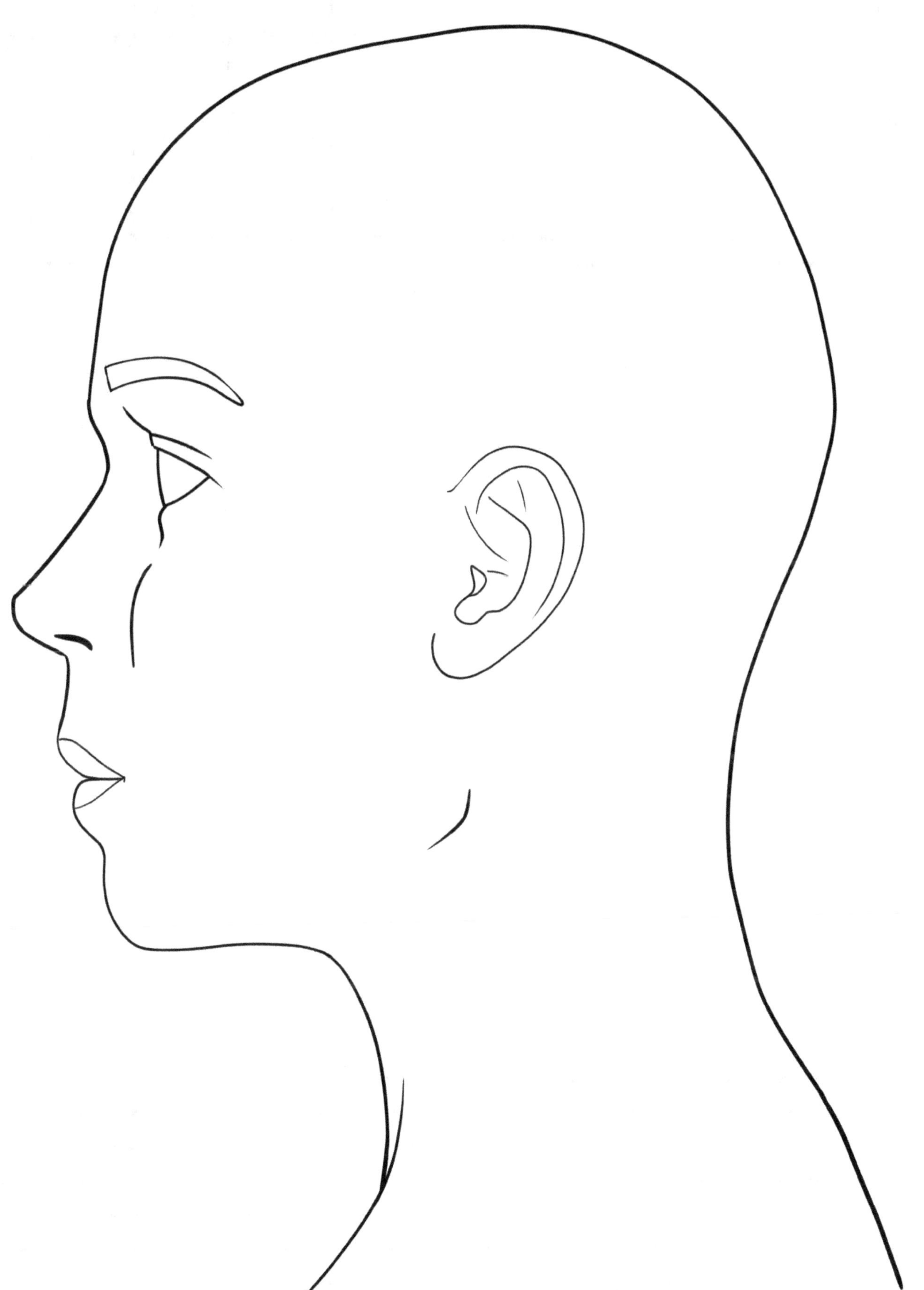

Client Name:

Placement:

Theme:

Planned Date:

Palette

Design:

Details / Notes:

Name ______________________________ Date ____________________

Left Side View Head/Neck Sketch Template

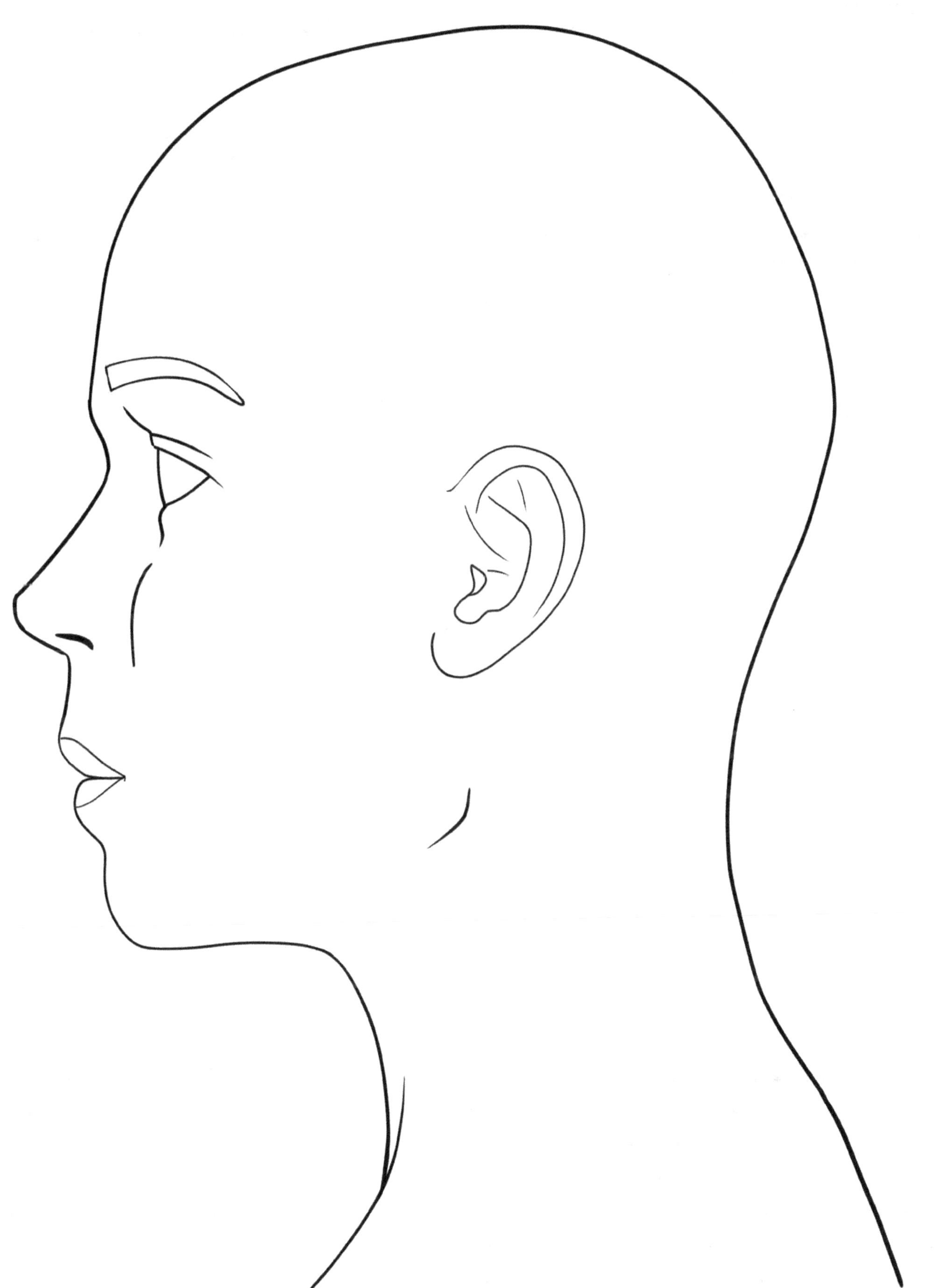

Client Name:

Placement:

Theme:

Planned Date:

Palette

Design:

Details / Notes:

Name ______________________________ Date ____________________

Left Side View Head/Neck Sketch Template

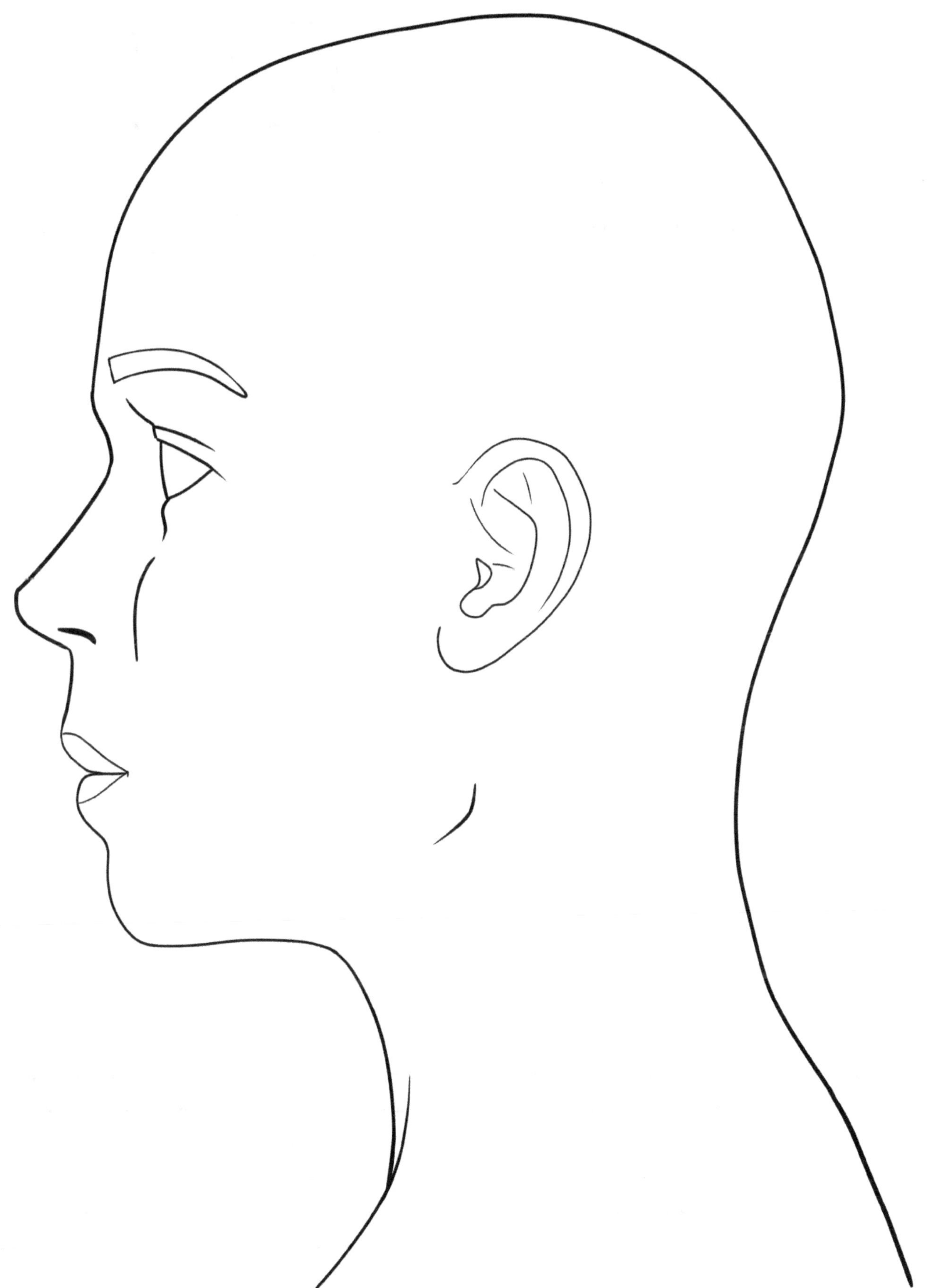

Client Name:

Placement:

Palette

Theme:

Planned Date:

Design:

Details / Notes:

Name ______________________________ Date ____________________

Left Side View Head/Neck Sketch Template

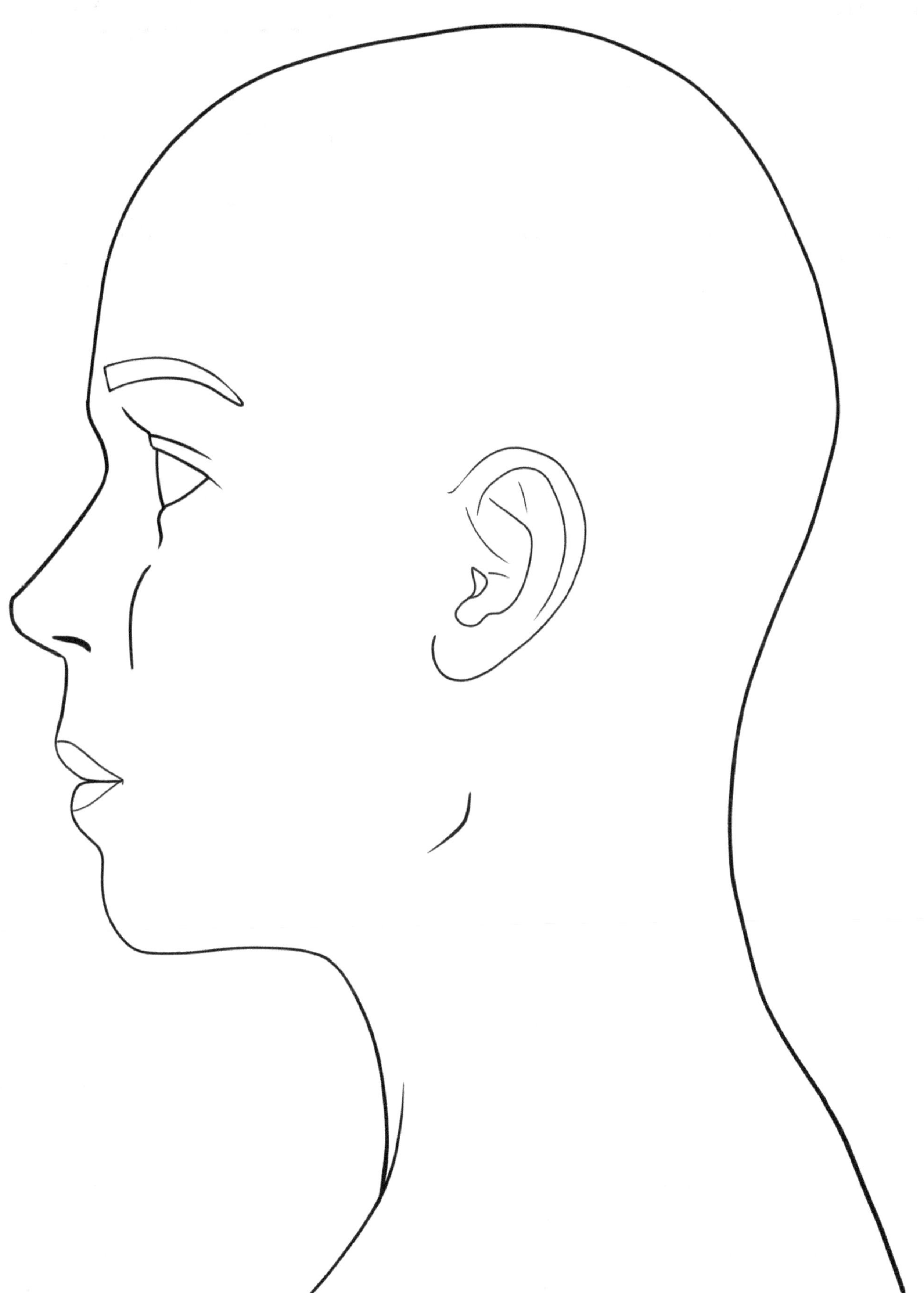

Client Name:

Placement:

Theme:

Planned Date:

Palette

Design:

Details / Notes:

Name ______________________________ Date ____________________

Left Side View Head/Neck Sketch Template

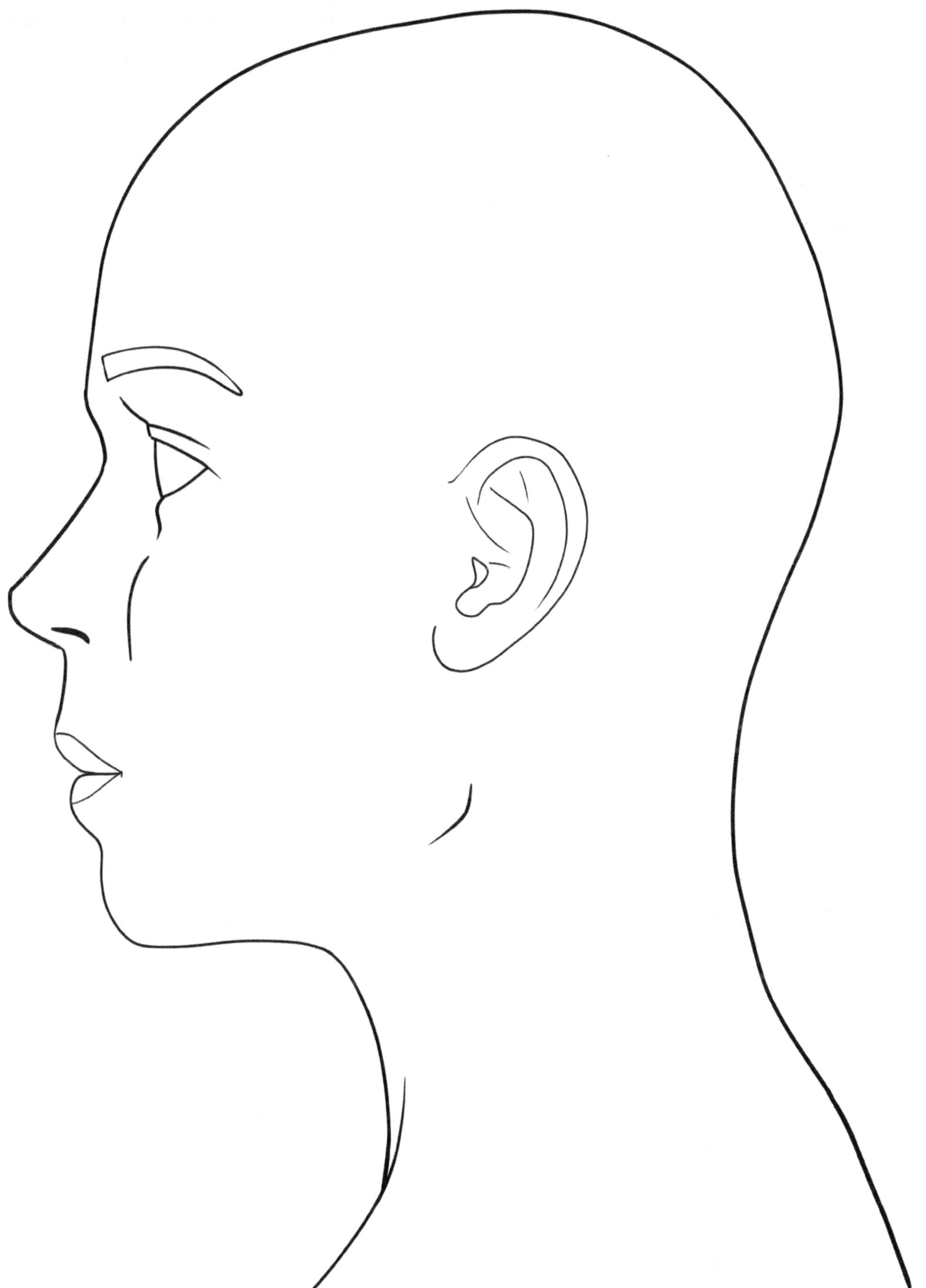

Client Name:

Placement:

Theme:

Planned Date:

Palette

Design:

Details / Notes:

Name ______________________________ Date ____________________

Left Side View Head/Neck Sketch Template

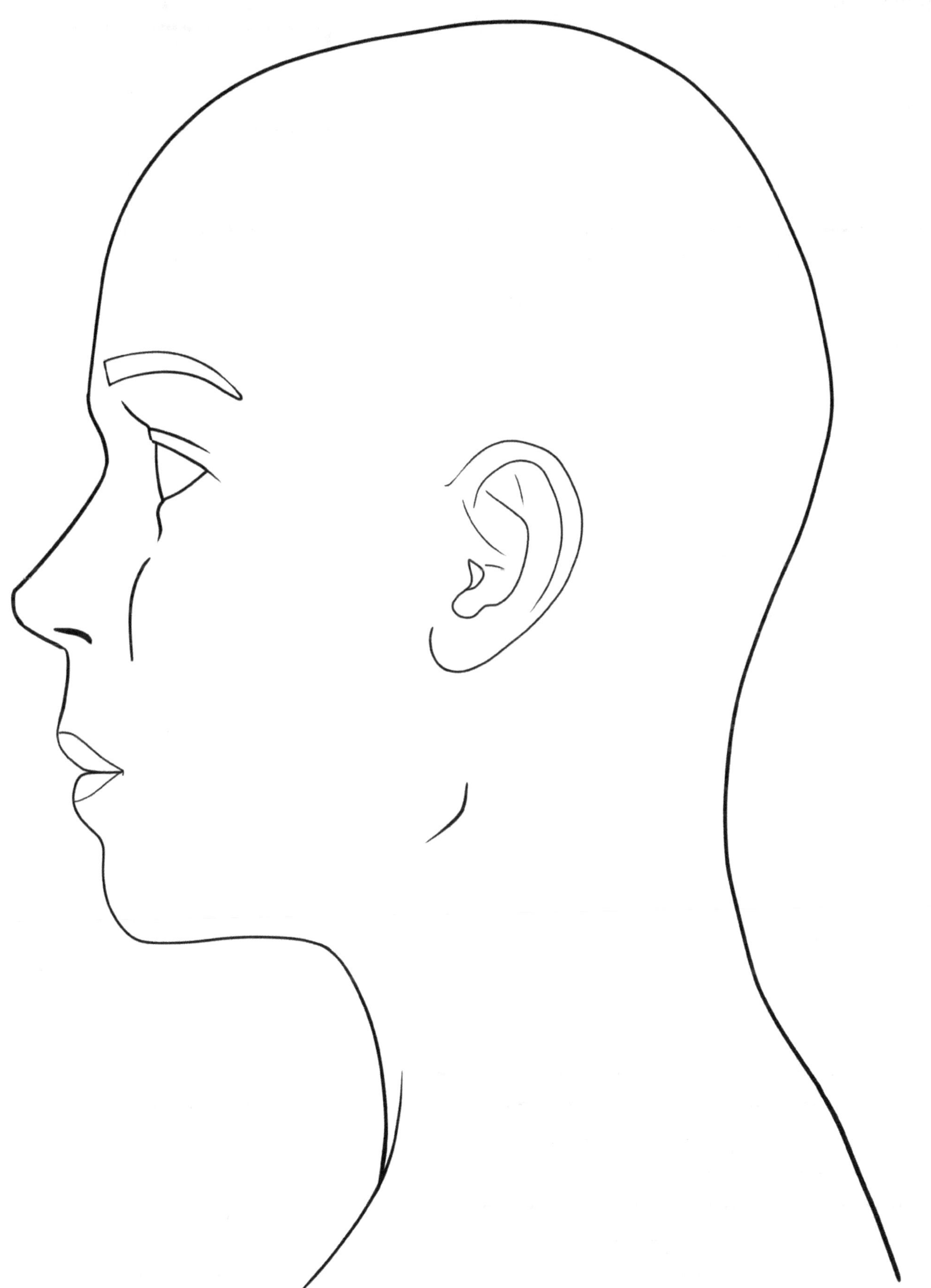

Client Name:

Placement:

Palette

Theme:

Planned Date:

Design:

Details / Notes:

Name ______________________________ Date ____________________

Left Side View Head/Neck Sketch Template

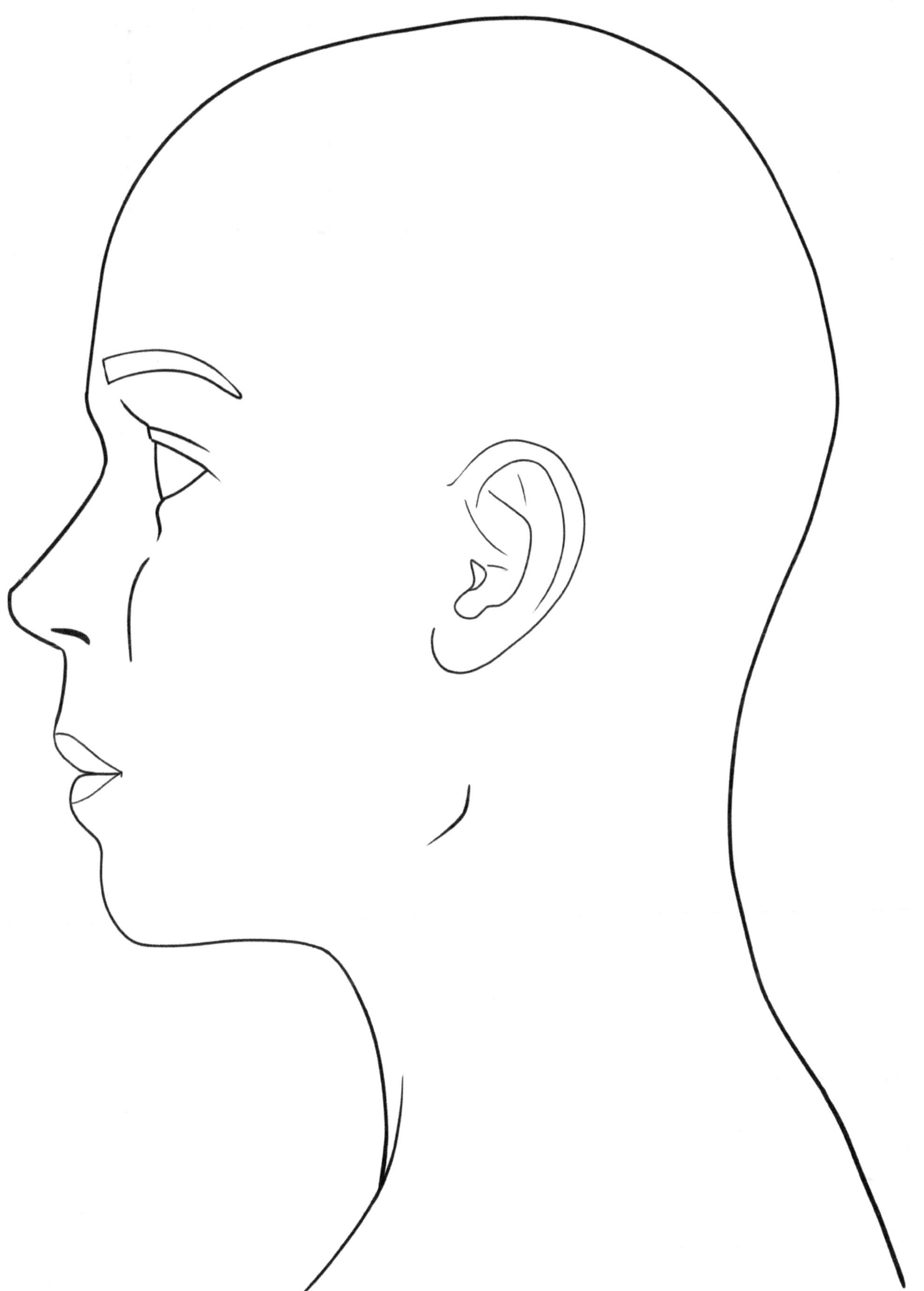

Client Name:

Placement:

Theme:

Planned Date:

Palette

Design:

Details / Notes:

Name ______________________________ Date ____________________

Left Side View Head/Neck Sketch Template

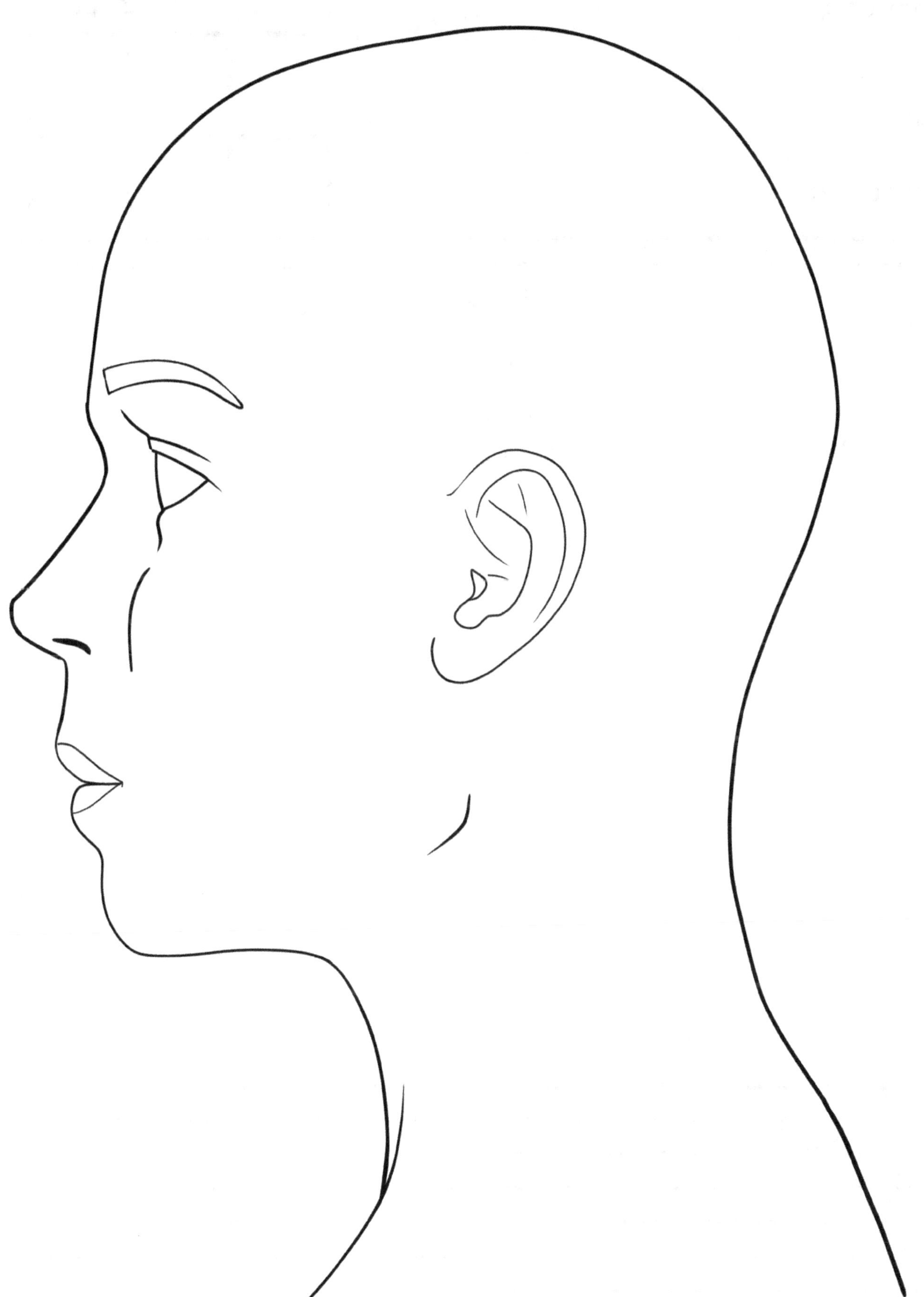

Client Name:

Placement:

Palette

Theme:

Planned Date:

Design:

Details / Notes:

Name ______________________________ Date ____________________ 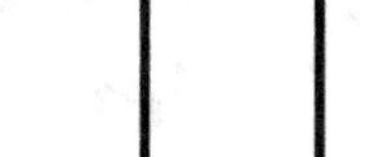

Left Side View Head/Neck Sketch Template

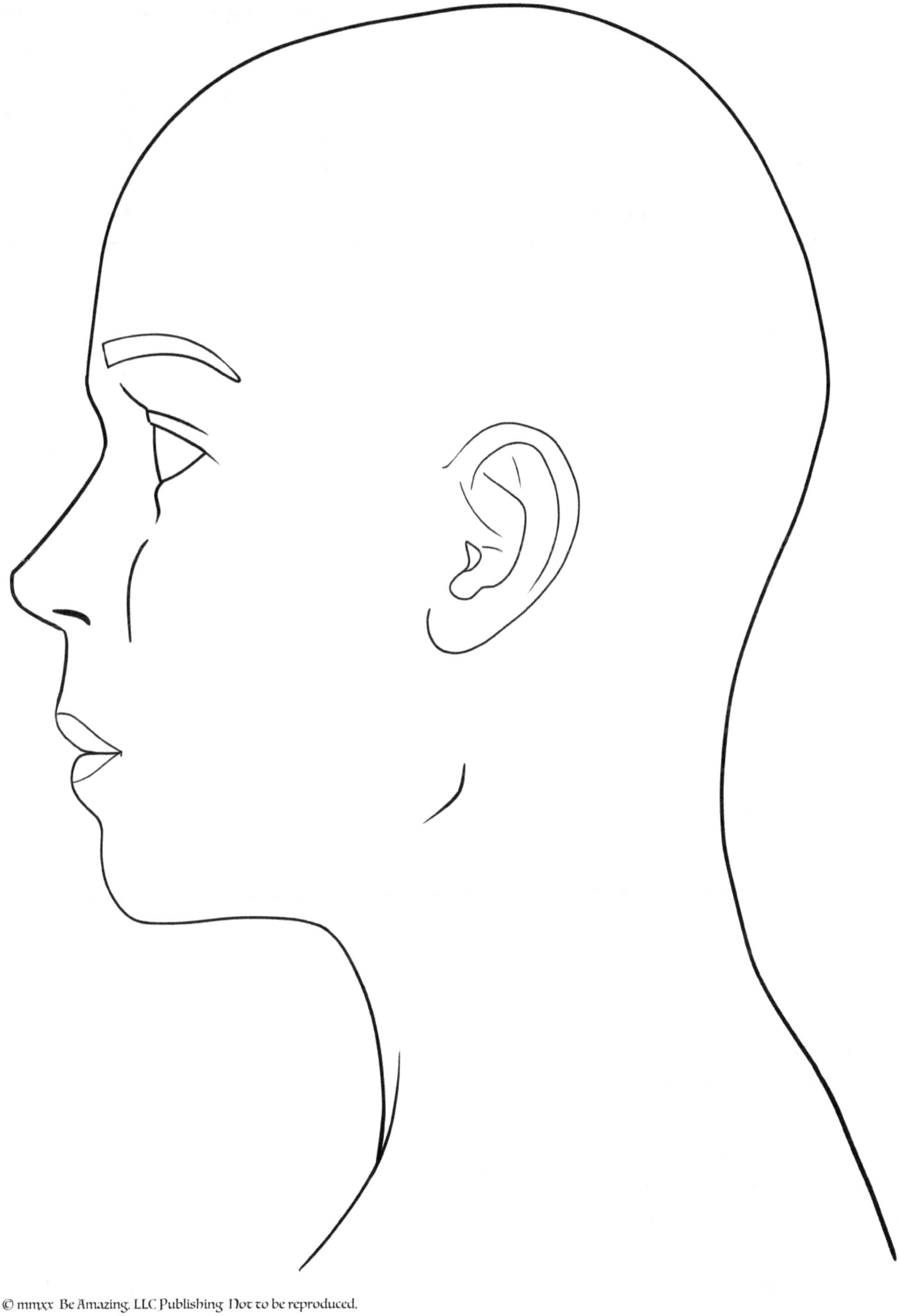

Client Name:

Placement:

Theme:

Planned Date:

Palette

Design:

Details / Notes:

Name ______________________________ Date ____________________

Right Side View Head/Neck Sketch Template

Client Name:

Placement:

Palette

Theme:

Planned Date:

Design:

Details / Notes:

Name ______________________________ Date ____________________

Right Side View Head/Neck Sketch Template

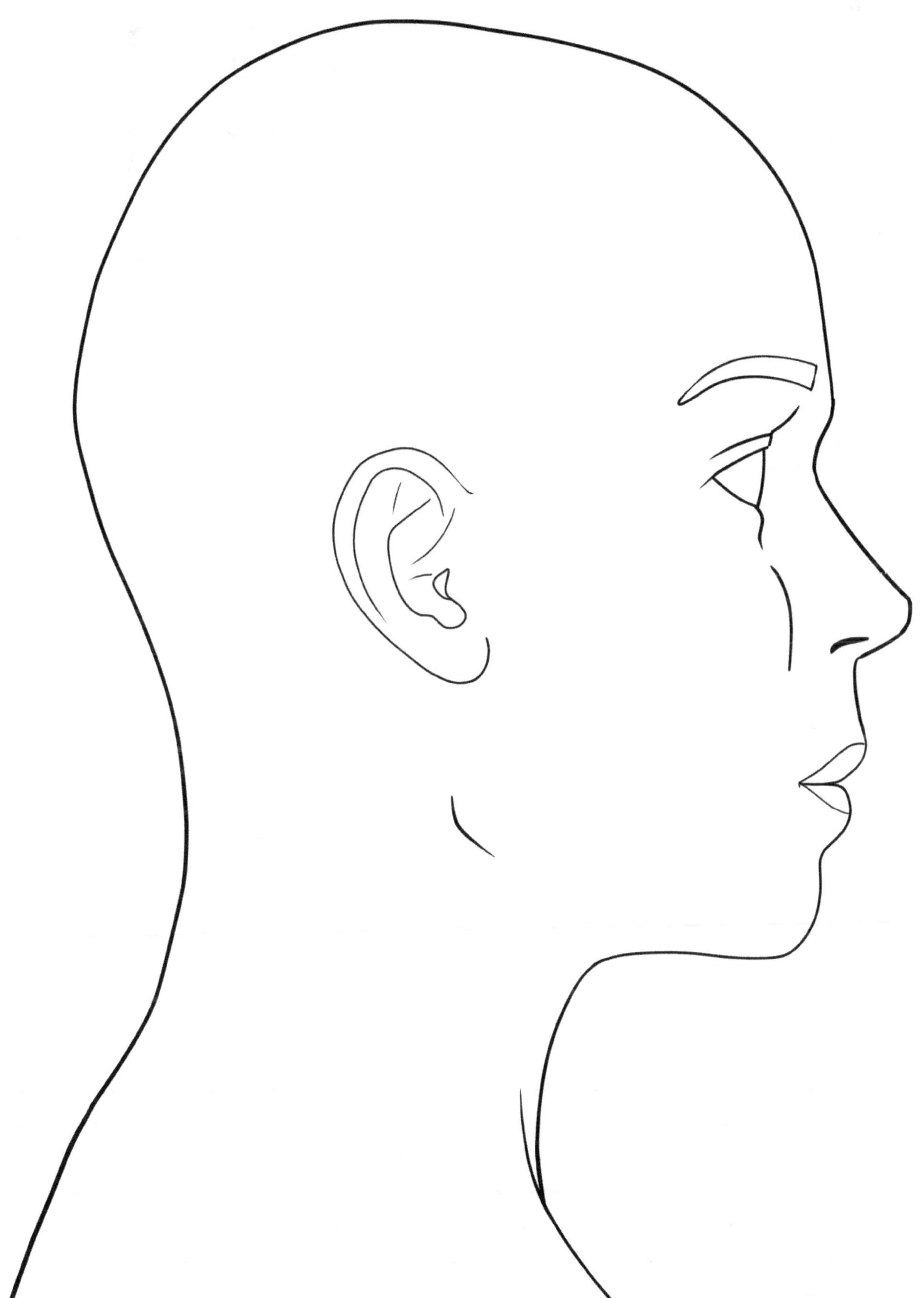

Client Name:

Placement:

Palette

Theme:

Planned Date:

Design:

Details / Notes:

Name ______________________________ Date ____________________

Right Side View Head/Neck Sketch Template

Client Name:

Placement:

Theme:

Planned Date:

Palette			

Design:

Details / Notes:

Name ______________________________ Date ____________________

Right Side View Head/Neck Sketch Template

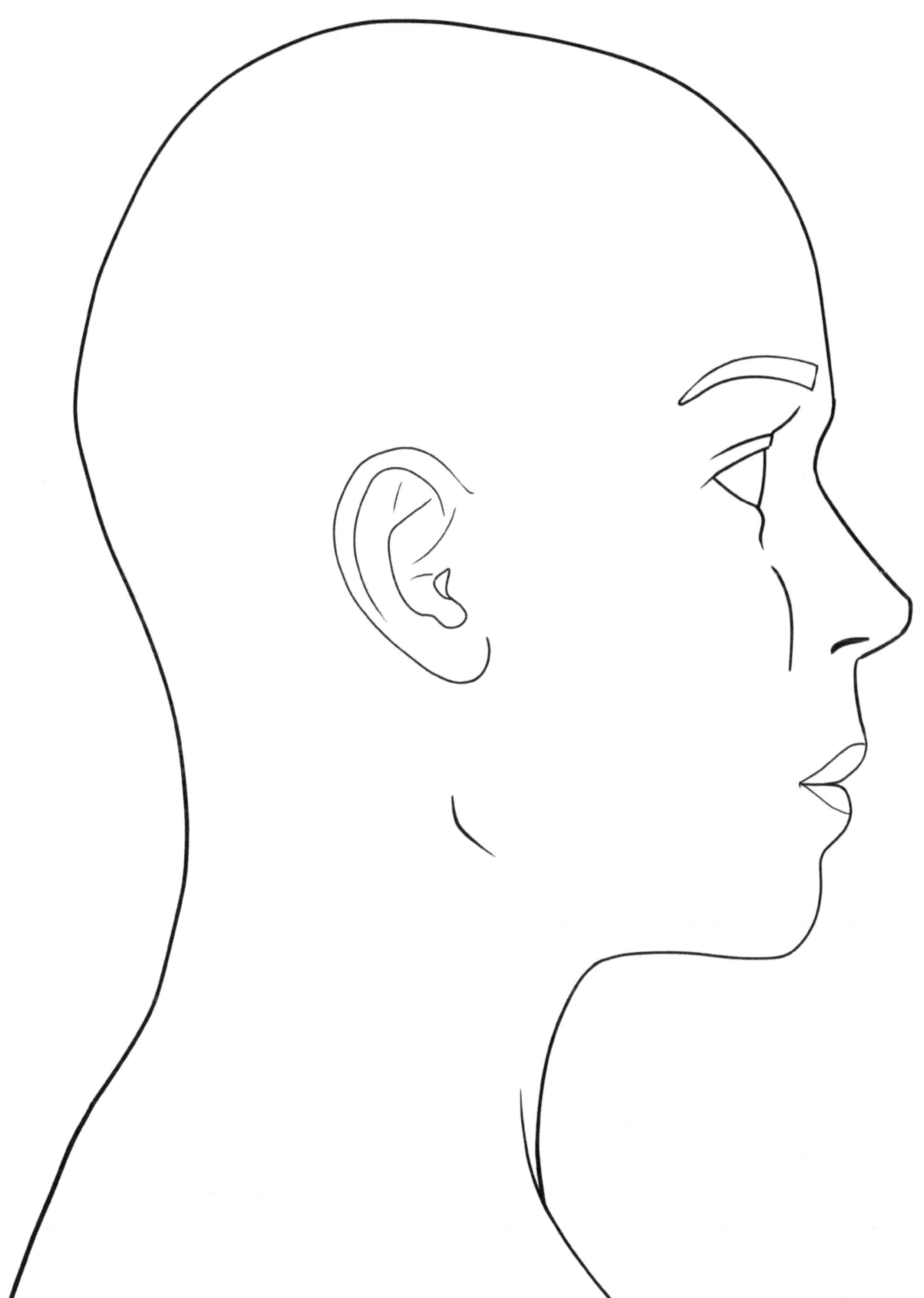

Client Name:

Placement:

Theme:

Planned Date:

Palette

Design:

Details / Notes:

Name ______________________________ Date ____________________

Right Side View Head/Neck Sketch Template

Client Name:

Placement:

Theme:

Planned Date:

Palette

Design:

Details / Notes:

Name ______________________________ Date ____________________

Right Side View Head/Neck Sketch Template

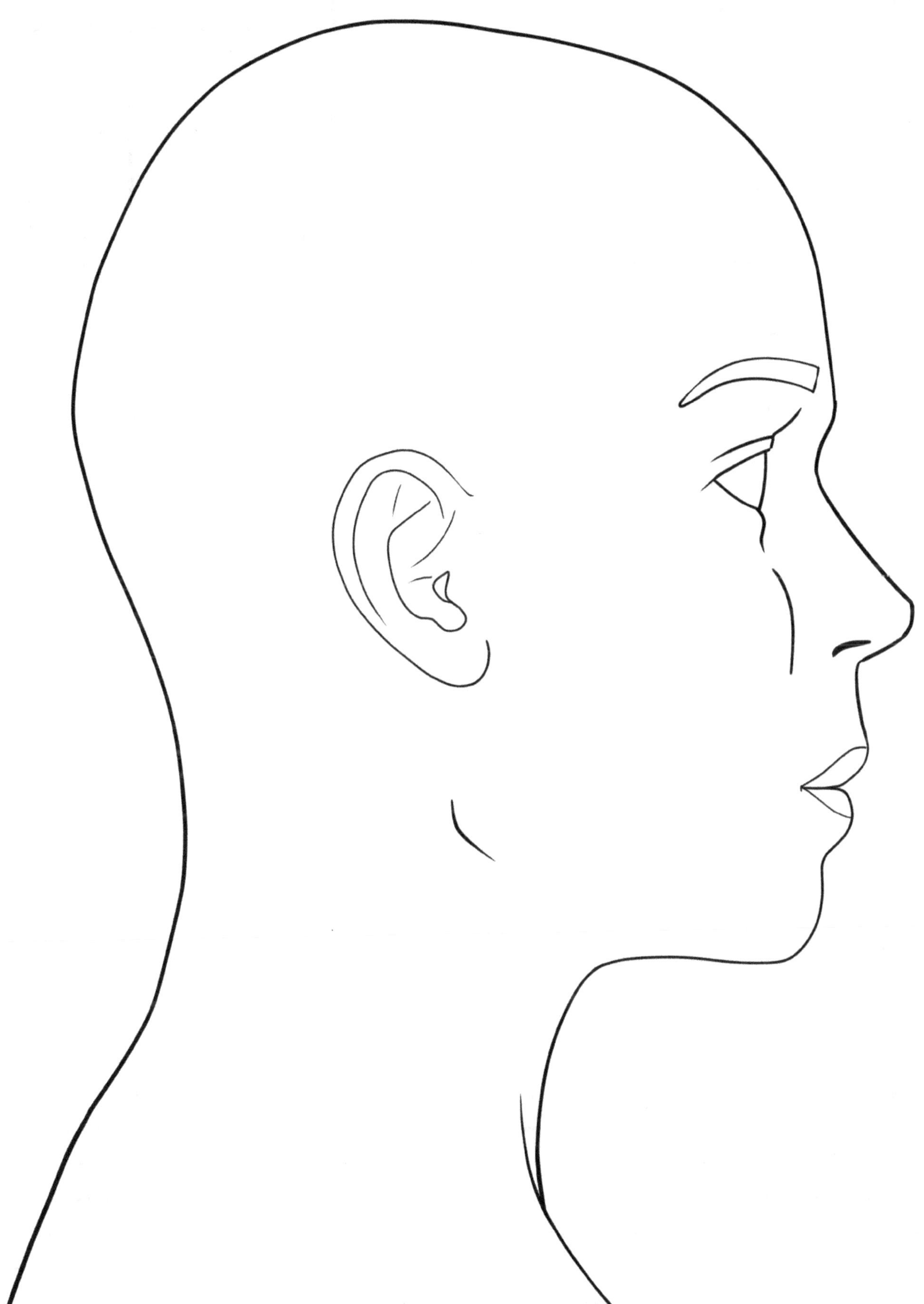

Client Name:

Placement:

Theme:

Planned Date:

Palette

Design:

Details / Notes:

Name ______________________________ Date ____________________

Right Side View Head/Neck Sketch Template

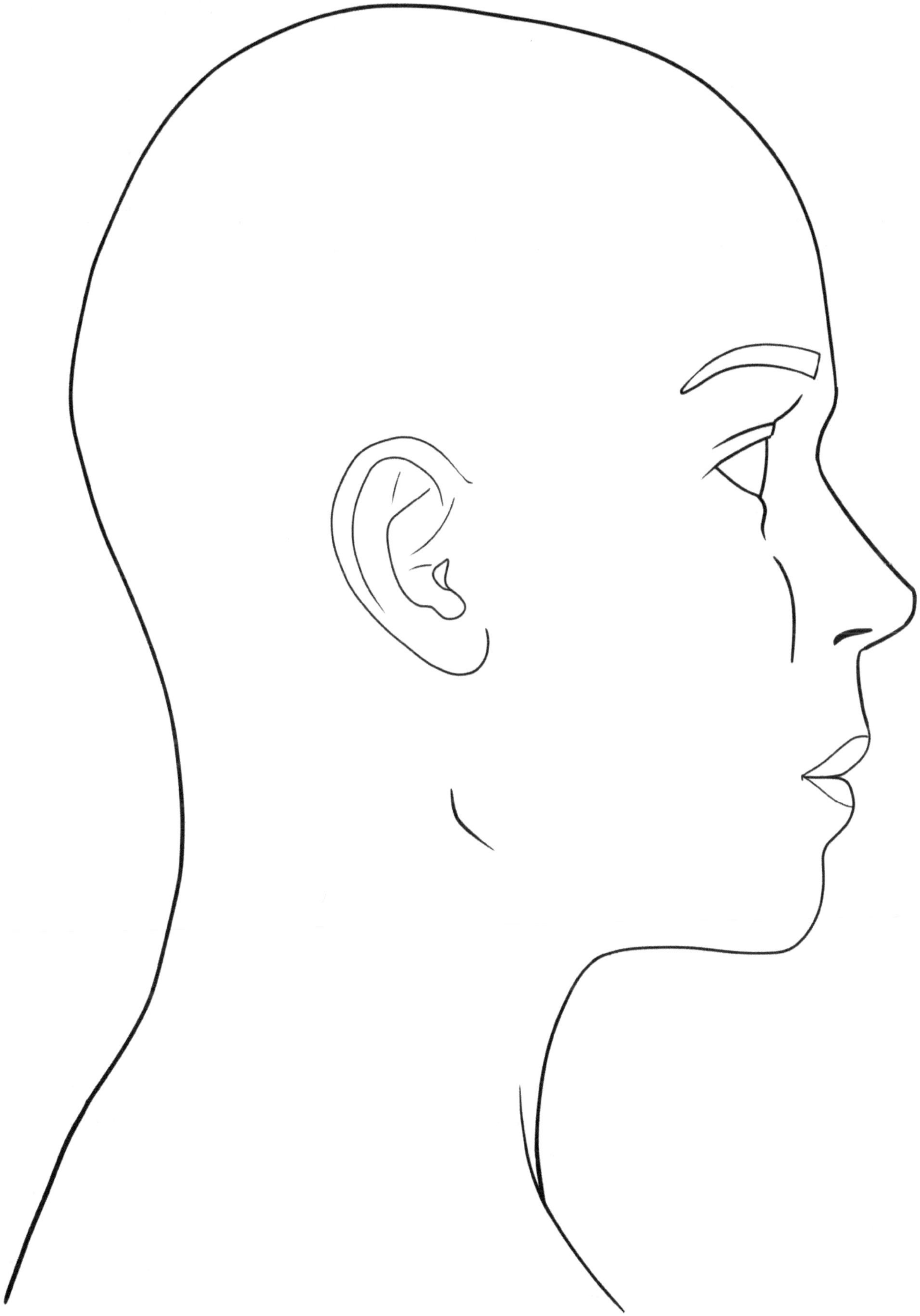

Client Name:

Placement:

Palette

Theme:

Planned Date:

Design:

Details / Notes:

Name ______________________________ Date ____________________

Right Side View Head/Neck Sketch Template

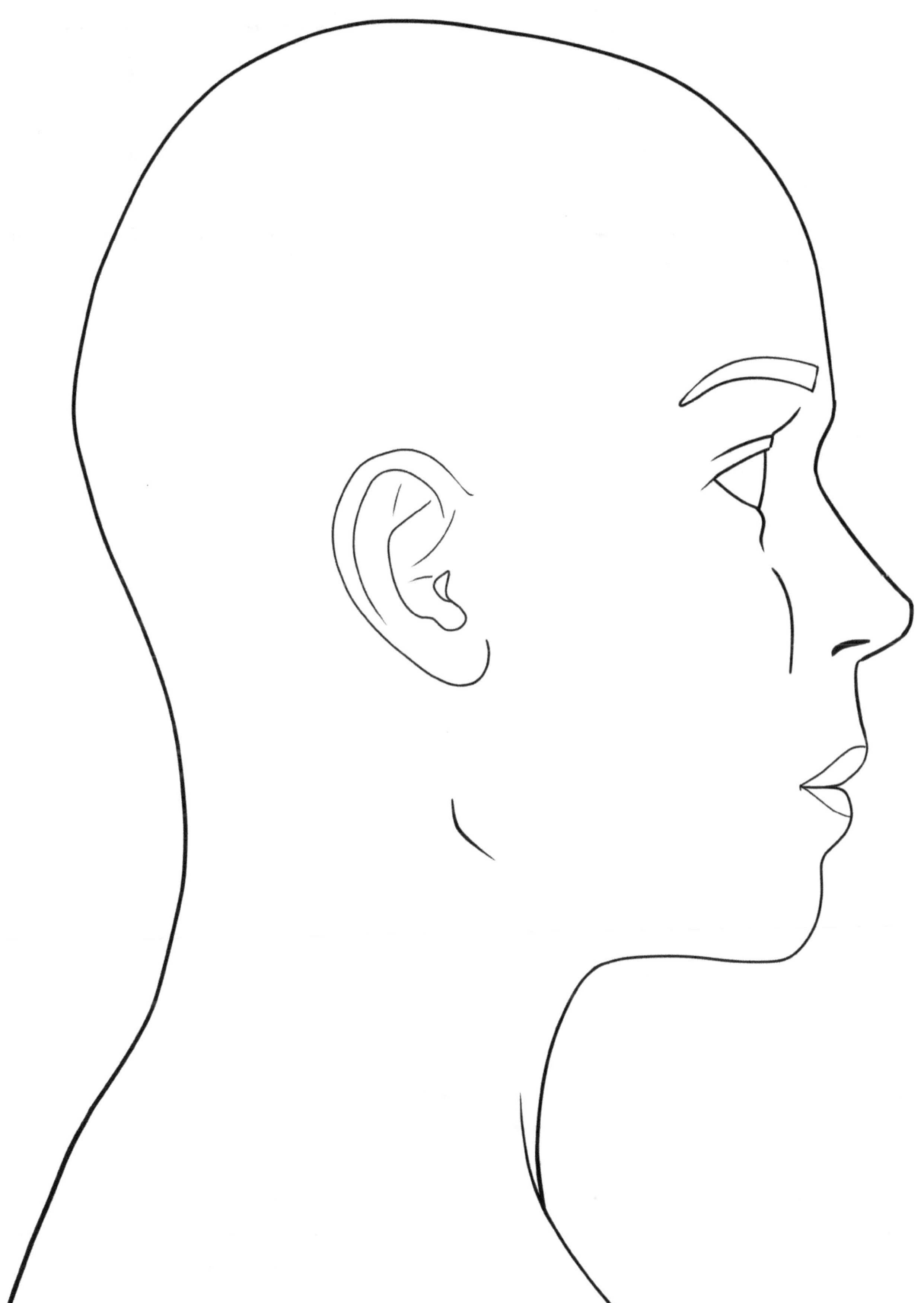

Client Name:

Placement:

Theme:

Planned Date:

Palette

Design:

Details / Notes:

Name ______________________________ Date ____________________

Right Side View Head/Neck Sketch Template

Client Name:

Placement:

Theme:

Planned Date:

Palette

Design:

Details / Notes:

Name ______________________________ Date ____________________

Right Side View Head/Neck Sketch Template

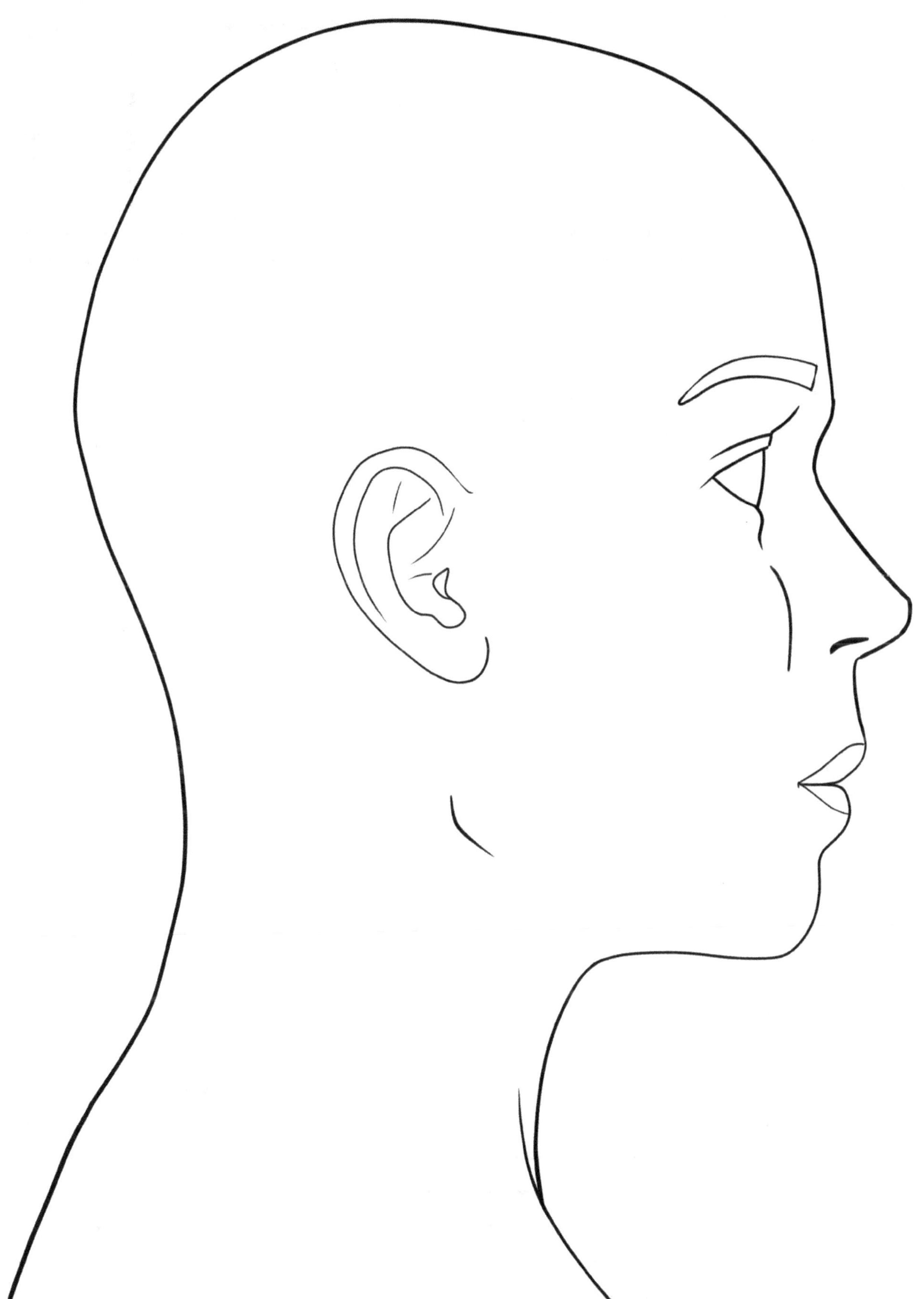

Client Name:

Placement:

Theme:

Planned Date:

Palette

Design:

Details / Notes:

Name ______________________________ Date ____________________

Right Side View Head/Neck Sketch Template

Client Name:

Placement:

Theme:

Planned Date:

Palette

Design:

Details / Notes:

Name ____________________________ Date ___________________

Right Side View Head/Neck Sketch Template

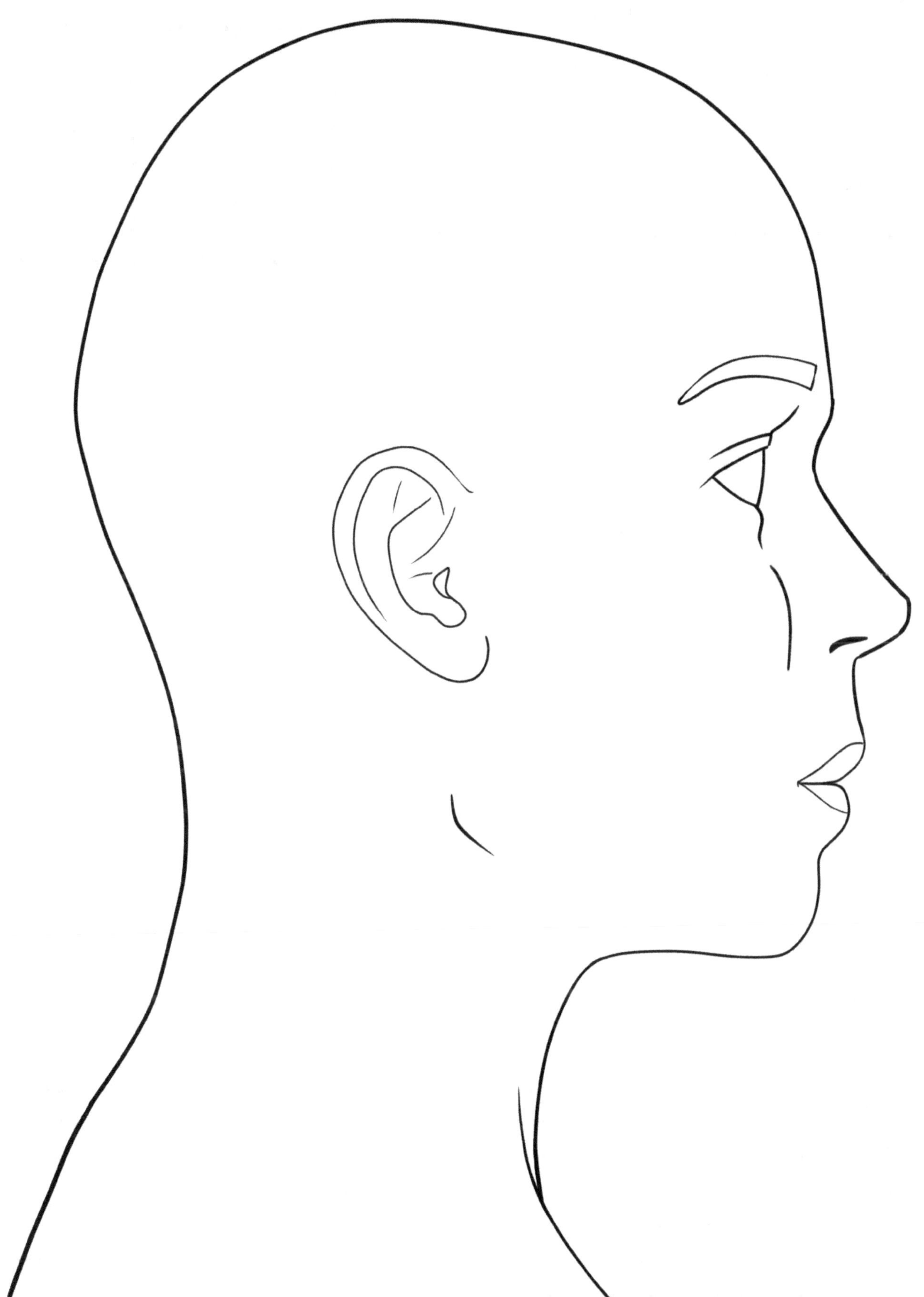

Client Name:

Placement:

Theme:

Planned Date:

Palette

Design:

Details / Notes:

Name ______________________ Date ________________

Right Side View Head/Neck Sketch Template

Client Name:

Placement:

Theme:

Planned Date:

Palette

Design:

Details / Notes:

Name ______________________________ Date ____________________

Rear View Head/Neck Sketch Template

Client Name:

Placement:

Theme:

Planned Date:

Palette

Design:

Details / Notes:

Name ______________________________ Date ____________________

Rear View Head/Neck Sketch Template

Client Name:

Placement:	Palette			
Theme:				
Planned Date:				

Design:

Details / Notes:

Name ______________________________ Date ____________________

Rear View Head/Neck Sketch Template

Client Name:

Placement:

Theme:

Planned Date:

Palette

Design:

Details / Notes:

Name ______________________________ Date ____________________

Rear View Head/Neck Sketch Template

Client Name:

Placement:

Theme:

Planned Date:

Palette

Design:

Details / Notes:

Name ______________________________ Date ____________________

Rear View Head/Neck Sketch Template

Client Name:

Placement:

Theme:

Planned Date:

Palette

Design:

Details / Notes:

Name ______________________________ Date ____________________

Rear View Head/Neck Sketch Template

Client Name:

Placement:

Palette

Theme:

Planned Date:

Design:

Details / Notes:

Name ______________________________ Date ____________________

Rear View Head/Neck Sketch Template

Client Name:

Placement:

Theme:

Planned Date:

Palette

Design:

Details / Notes:

Name ______________________________ Date ____________________

Rear View Head/Neck Sketch Template

Client Name:

Placement:

Palette

Theme:

Planned Date:

Design:

Details / Notes:

Name ______________________________ Date ____________________

Rear View Head/Neck Sketch Template

Client Name:

Placement:

Theme:

Planned Date:

Palette

Design:

Details / Notes:

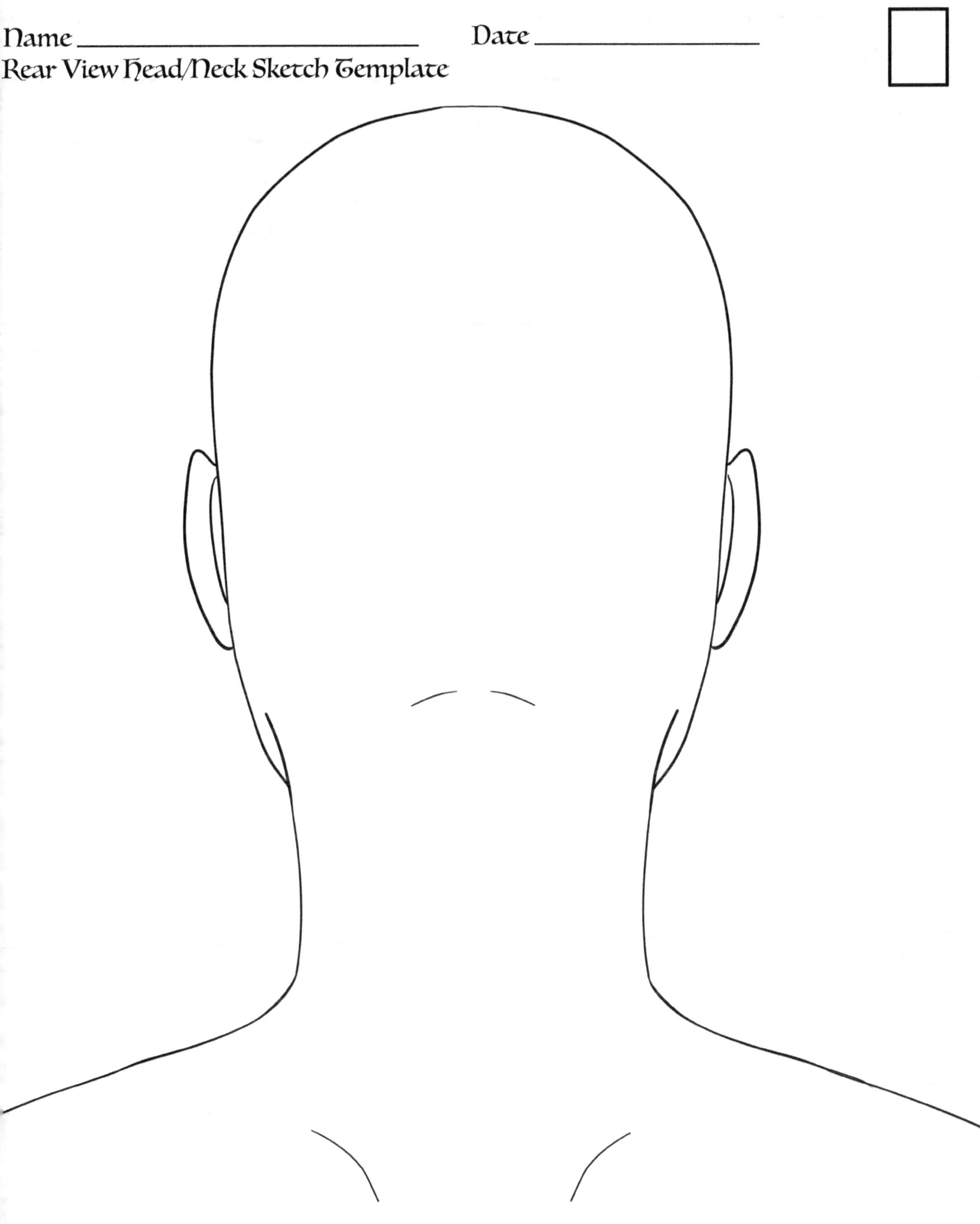
Name
Date
Rear View Head/Neck Sketch Template

Client Name:

Placement:

Theme:

Planned Date:

Palette			

Design:

Details / Notes:

Name ______________________________ Date ____________________

Rear View Head/Neck Sketch Template

Client Name:

Placement:

Theme:

Planned Date:

Palette

Design:

Details / Notes:

Name ______________________________ Date ____________________

Rear View Head/Neck Sketch Template

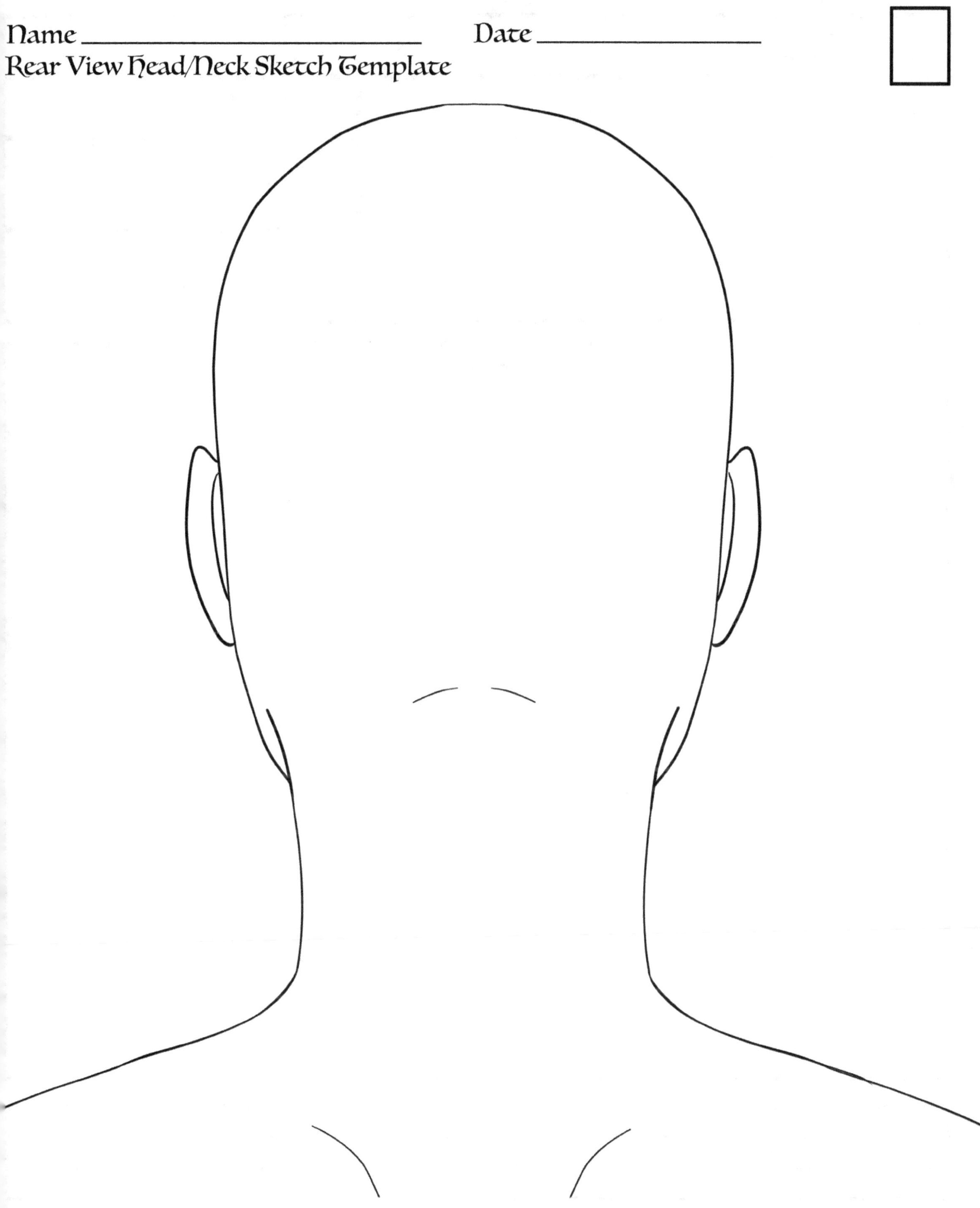

Client Name:

Placement:

Theme:

Planned Date:

Palette			

Design:

Details / Notes:

Name ______________________________ Date ____________________

Rear View Head/Neck Sketch Template

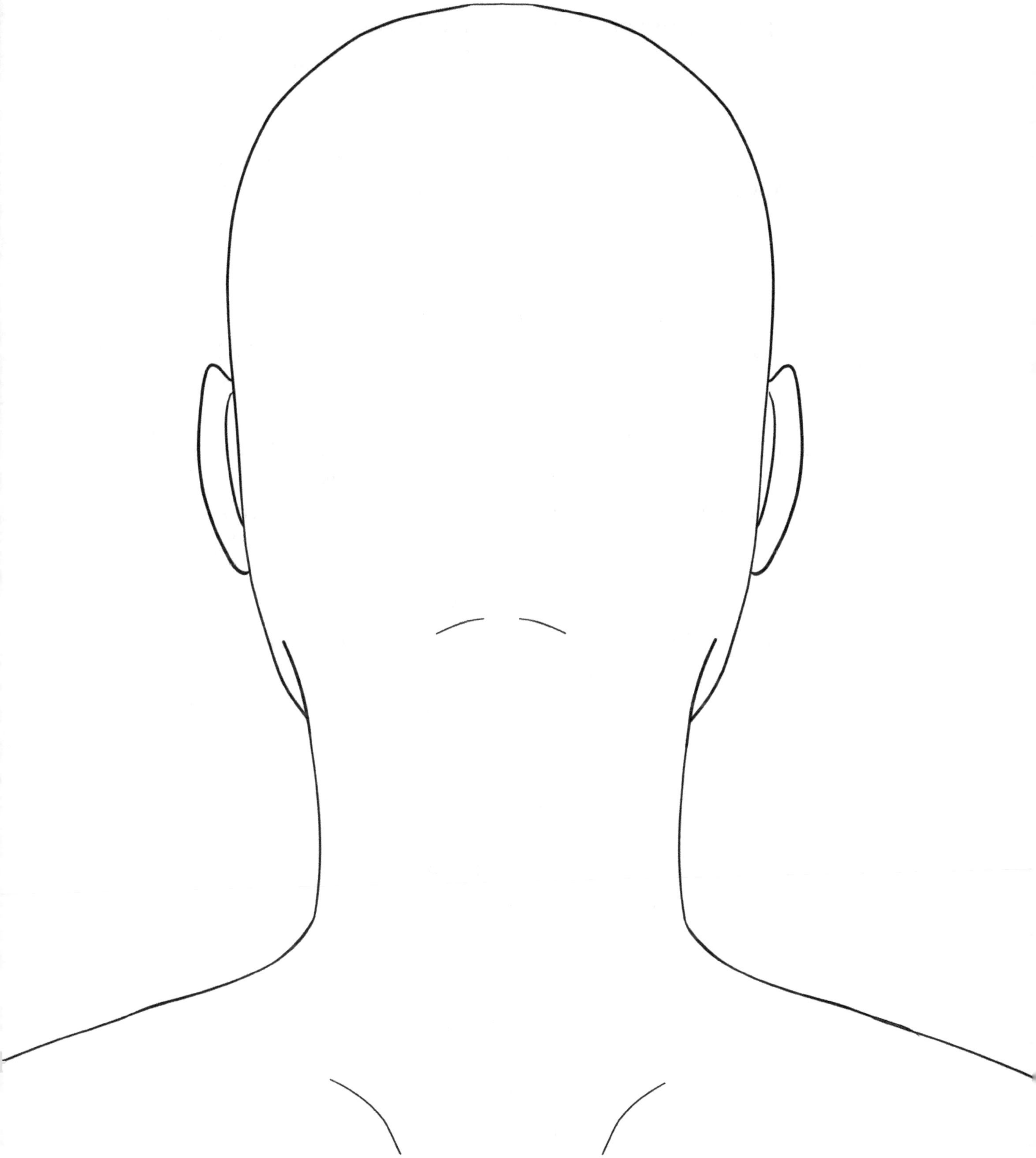

Thank You...
...for purchasing our Tattoo Sketchbook and Journal VI
Check out other sketchbooks designed
by Tangie Marie and Cameron Purvis.

Blank Comic Sketchbook 200 Bright White Pages
Blank Comic Sketchbook 100 Bright White Pages

Blank Storyboard Sketchbook
Featuring 16:9 Thumbnail Panels 200 Bright White Pages
Blank Storyboard Sketchbook
Featuring 16:9 Thumbnail Panels 100 Bright White Pages

Blank Storyboard Sketchbook
Featuring 4:3Thumbnail Panels 200 Bright White Pages
Blank Storyboard Sketchbook
Featuring 4:3 Thumbnail Panels 100 Bright White Pages

Blank Storyboard Sketchbook
Featuring 1:1 Thumbnail Panels 200 Bright White Pages
Blank Storyboard Sketchbook
Featuring 1:1 Thumbnail Panels 100 Bright White Pages

Blank Tattoo Journal and Sketchbook
Tattoo Journal and Sketchbook
Tattoo Sketchbook and Journal
Tattoo Sketchbook and Journal IV
Tattoo Sketchbook and Journal V

Need a children's book?
We have those too.
Check out these titles:
Alexander Ant and the Art Contest
Goodnight, Meow
The 12 Nights of Winter

www.ingramcontent.com/pod-product-compliance
Lightning Source LLC
LaVergne TN
LVHW061250100826
845148LV00008B/1081

* 9 7 8 1 7 3 6 0 7 9 6 4 5 *